Programmed for
Failure

Programmed for Failure

a Triptych

Herbert Wieder, M.D.

Authors Choice Press
San Jose New York Lincoln Shanghai

Programmed for Failure
a Triptych

Authors Choice Press
an imprint of iUniverse.com, Inc.

For information address:
iUniverse.com, Inc.
5220 S 16th, Ste. 200
Lincoln, NE 68512
www.iuniverse.com

ISBN: 0-595-19438-9

Printed in the United States of America

Contents

Acknowledgements

Thanks to
Laurance Wieder, for letting me interrupt him as needed
Jonna Brasch Wieder, for all kinds of support
Tom Delgiacco, for generous loan of his sharp eyes

Prologue

"The time has come," the walrus said, "to talk of many things"(14). About how a day doesn't pass without media highlighting the inexorable escalation of society's problems and the community's demands to find "basic causes" to each of them. About multi-billion dollar expenditures on mass-oriented programs that promised solutions to knotty, tangled problems of illiteracy, drug abuse, adolescent indiscipline. And about how they failed to unravel or even loosen them.

Because of their failure to perform, these programs have provoked serious public criticisms about their costs and value. As remedies to the non-performing ventures, more programs that have the seeds of failure already in them are proposed. This is something like the halt following the lame! It is not more programs that are needed, we shall see, but explanations of why the current ones failed. I believe that the roots of the failed programs are imbedded in flawed theories which I intend to examine. That is what this communication is all about. I don't intend to join the crowd of social reformers who offer overly optimistic, unrealistic claims for non-existent cure-all programs. Bitter experience has taught me as a knowledgeable professional that no single-minded answers for mass-oriented programs for easy victories exist.

What will be highlighted could easily be applied to many other existing non-performing programs.

My professional experience in the fields of drugs, adolescence, and learning problems, which I have chosen to discuss, permit me to express my views with some degree of force, even if controversial and inflammatory. Since I am addressing the general public, I have attempted to keep scientific terms, more often confusing than explanatory, to a minimum or clarified by translating them into every daylanguage. Although I take a few liberties with language, I ask forbearance because of my good intention to clarify. At the same time, a discussion of scientific topics needs some taste of its jargon.

The public's call for "basic causes" conjures the "Trials of Hercules" (116). Hera, Goddess of Life, sister and wife to Zeus, was murderously jealous of any woman, divine or mortal, who won Zeus's interest. The children of Zeus's mistresses, notably Hercules the son of Zeus and the mortal princess Alcemene, suffered her rage. Hera had originally sent two serpents to kill Hercules when he was a child, but instead he killed the snakes. Later in his life, duped by a fit of "madness" induced by Hera, Hercules killed his wife Meagra and their children. As punishment, he was commanded by the oracle at Delphi to perform Twelve Labors, one of which was to slay the deadly Hydra. Others before Hercules had tried and failed because the Hydra's dangerous heads when cut off would immediately regenerate. Discovering that one head possessed immortal energy that was energizing the regeneration of the decapitated heads, Hercules triumphed by decapitating that head first, burying it, and sealing the cut with fire. Then he cut off the remaining heads which were unable to regenerate. The "basic causes" of the serpent's dangerous qualities were not in the individual mortal heads, but in the singular secret force in the immortal head. Not until that head was destroyed could the Hydra be neutralized. That myth bears relating to modern society's search for the "many basic causes" of its problems: "Do the numerous destructive social problems develop from many basic causes or from a common, shared cause?"

My basic premise is that problems are born of Man who creates and perpetuates them, but shrinks from self-incriminating, self-criticizing explanations of causation, preferring causal theories which point away from himself. Hence the seductive appeal of "socioeconomic," "politico-economic," "poverty-crime" theories. A cosmic theory blaming it all on sunspots would be even more satisfying. The more distance from vanity-bruising revelations of his irrationalities the better, for few would accept a proposition that the "basic causes" of society's problems stem from one "root cause," Man himself.

About theories and strategies

Every therapeutic program, or strategy, is derived from a theory which is an informed but tentative statement, "a guess," about the relationship of observed events (90). Confirmed or disproved only by empirical observations, a theory must be consistent with other established theories relevant to the subject and possess a capability for prediction. If new conflicting data are found, or if predictions from the theory are ultimately proved incorrect, the theory must be amended or discarded. All of the empirical findings from which a theory was derived are retained however; only theories, the guesses, are abandoned. Accurate definitions in a valid theoretical underpinning must be the basis of the derived strategy, or the program will fail from the start. Flawed theories that seduce strategists into expensive failures, can result from many causes which include inaccurate definitions, along with unrealistic goals, misconceptions, unproven opinions, and the disregard of previous, relevant, clinical scientific studies.

Knowing history, the sayings go, should prevent recurring expenditures of time, energy, and money on more of the same! Or, "He who is ignorant of the past is doomed to repeat it." I consider it is relevant and important to present as background knowledge, the historical data that should have been integrated into the planning of the current programs but had been disregarded. History will show the past's contributions to program failures and hopefully will undo some of the widespread misinformation and misconceptions prevalent that mislead society. History will further underscore how the man-made flaws in the theories behind the failed programs arose and skeptics may see the validity of the criticisms of the programs.

Knowing something about the complex structuring of various problems will enlighten the interested person about how mental functions normally develop from the impact of the external environment on innate biological givens. Microscopic examination of the failed programs will reveal that by not including psychological factors as causal environmental forces, inexperienced planners failed to recognize that the non-inclusion functioned as an obstruction to the successful implementation of programs. Eventually the repeated failures forced the consideration of psychological factors as a cause. Then, as the complexity of the problems became imprinted in the researcher's awareness, "cure" seemed a long way off. To paraphrase Freud, (35) "Even if we could not see solutions clearly we could at least see clearly what the obstacles were."

1

The Drug Scene

History of the birth of drugs

We must take a sober look at the drug scene. Drugs are in the public eye and the political arena. Public clamor that something must be done has forced the transfer of decision-making from the halls of science to the corridors of politics. Programs of treatment, prevention, and research—best designed with quiet, sensitive objectivity,—are buffeted by the winds of public alarm, missionary zeal, and political expediency.

Man's frailty has created another ecological disaster—the poisoning of his own body! Some startling statistics gathered by a New York state survey in 1967-68, foretold the current "abusive use explosion." In a state population of fourteen million, over one-half million people used tranquilizers regularly; 377,000 took barbiturates at least six times monthly; one quarter million took diet pills (amphetamines) on a regular basis; 50,000 took LSD and 41,000 took heroin at least six times monthly! The public's attitude at that time was that drugs were a perfectly acceptable means of coping with stress. These numbers have soared since 1968 along with the hope that discovery of a new miracle drug remains alive; "the mind is always prone to believe what it wishes to be true": a magic potion must exist (50).

We need to know how and why "drugs" first appeared on the human horizon. Why do drugs exist? Why are they used and abused? What can be done? What cannot be done? Obviously hard, prehistoric evidence is lacking about the "birth of drugs"; therefore only enlightened conjecture may be offered. Alcohol could have been discovered by chance when primitive Firstman found a pool of rotten, fermented fruits, and while eating and drinking from it, he experienced feelings that he wished to repeat. Curiosity stimulated trial and error experimentation with many substances found or concocted, so that, over millennia, substances that altered mind and body functions accrued.

Drugs did not suddenly appear unheralded or unknown to the world. Ancient documents, bibles, historical and literary works from Shakespeare, deQuincy, the Borgias, Sleeping Beauty, Cinderella, and countless other works in modern literature confirm Man's early awareness of what he originally called "herbals, poisons, and potions." Defined at first by their effects, which were attributed to "magic mixed in by the gods," the substances were collectively called "drugs" centuries later (74). "Drugs," substances by any name, were born of Man, the only animal that deliberately creates and uses them to serve his wishes or needs. The modern proliferation of "drugs" erupted from the same source that produced them in the first place. This is a simple statement of fact about the "epidemic of drugs" which seems such an enigma to the public at large. The spectacular diversification of substances and their uses that have occurred since antiquity is not surprising. The market, the means, and the human motivation to expand have been there all along.

Early references to substances (98)

In Sumerian cuneiform writings dating from 4000 B.C. the poppy was called "the plant of joy." The juice of the poppy was extolled in Assyrian medical tablets of the 7th century B.C. (98). Opium had been called the "Gift of the Gods," while morphine, one of its later derivatives, was labelled "God's own medicine." Homer wrote that Helen of Troy "cast into the wine a potion to quiet all pain and bring forgetfulness of every ill." In the Ebers Papyrus of Thebes of 1552 B.C. a mixture of opium was recommended for quieting children whose crying disturbed their mothers. This was probably the first appearance of paregoric and "Mrs. Winslow's syrup." The Arabs, recognizing its marketing value, distributed opium over the world during the 10th and 11th centuries. A French naturalist, Pierre Belon, travelling extensively in the Orient in the 11th century, wrote, "There is no Turk who will not buy opium with his last coin and carry it with him in war and peace because it makes him have less fear."

Belief in magic: A universal factor in human thinking

Human belief in magic as a potent universal influence in mental functioning is also on record from ancient days up to modern studies. Childhood daydreams, night dreams, mass media hyperbole, fairy tales, and myths overflow with undisguised wishes for magic intervention of the "gods" for mastery of life and the world. Prayers, incantations, and wishes for substances to gratify passions, overcome pain, conquer fear, especially when ill or disturbed by life situations are commonplace.

Potions are sought to achieve love, beauty, health, wealth, eternal power, fertility, immortality, the Fountain of Youth a complete list would be a catalogue of every human wish and fear. Even in the 21st century many believers still attribute substances' effects to the "magic of the gods."

The ages of three to five are referred to as the "Magic Years" (28) because childhood thinking in that period of life, persisting unconsciously into adulthood, is characterized by "wishing makes it so." Human belief in magic created the imagined "medicine man," "witch doctor," and "alchemists" who practiced magic rituals and concocted potions promising various satisfactions. The title "Medicine Man" (15) designated a person, feared and revered, who possessed supernatural powers called "strong medicine" to influence peoples' lives. Artists and people in the performing arts were feared as well. The talents to capture a man's spirit by artists and to become someone else as actors was "strong medicine." The man of healing in the tribe, the "Witch Doctor," invoked and incanted magic to cure.

Modern patients often assess their physicians as "God-like" and endow them with personal qualities that blend the magic and wisdom of the Medicine Man with the talents of the Witch Doctor. One physician criticized for "playing God" retorted, "Every time a doctor gives a pill, he is playing God." Physicians may in fact achieve some of their therapeutic successes because their patients experience them as "God-like" (98). Religion itself has been called the "opiate of the people." Healing and killing magic, called obeah, voodoo, black magic and other designations, is practiced by revered chosen elders of many primitive cultures. The ultimate root of all therapies and pharmacology may be embedded in the belief in magic thought, the nutrient essence of wishes, dreams, myths, superstitions and prayer. "Magic," "medicine," and "drugs" have been linked in the human mind from the beginning of Man's consciousness.

Psychological attitudes and beliefs of adults, as we know, evolve from childhood influences (12). The extensive exposure to family, ethnic, and cultural medical lore during childhood, for example, creates the adult's concepts and behavior with "drugs," treatment, and doctors. The imprint into infantile memory of pleasurable, comforting experiences of "mother-breast-milk" may be the prototype for "drug" and "drug-like experiences." The argot in the drug scene unwittingly acknowledges this connection when users call their suppliers "mother" and their supplies "mood food." The soothing babies' pacifiers, thumbs, blankets, dolls, and other fetishes as symbolic contacts with "mother," are created out of baby needs and wishes for relief of tensions, contributing to further bonding of the concepts "drug" and "magic" (98).

Placebo

Many substances have well-recognized, even predictable, pharmacological effects on the mind. Yet anything that the user believes to have magical powers may also affect his state of mind even if the substance is chemically inert. A person can be convinced that a strong medicine is helping him when an inert solution containing a stinging element is applied to his skin. This is a familiar placebo effect, grounded in the takers' and/or givers' wishes and expectations. Research suggests that "magical thinking" may be the source of this well-documented but poorly understood human "placebo reaction." It influences health fads, cults, all therapies, and alternative medicine procedures (81). Scientifically confirmed, measurable, and predictable, placebo reactions are active in all chemical, physical, psychological, or ritual strategies. Harmful or helpful, effective or ineffective, depending on an unconscious faith in the substance, procedure, or provider, placebo reaction may create, enhance, or diminish a predicted therapeutic reaction. Highly sophisticated double-blind clinical studies can now estimate what an effective dose of an antibiotic substance should be. However, what is computed as effective in one clinic may be ineffective in another.

"Placebo reactions" show wide diversity. The godlike physician may prescribe a sugar pill to satisfy a patient's wish for medicine when none is needed and the patient feels "cured." An ethnic medication, chicken soup with matzoh balls, called "penicillin on the rocks" is claimed to be a cureall; copper bracelets are alleged to relieve orthopedic ailments; a lime on the forehead eases headache and does for many believers! Nobel Laureate Linus Pauling's "cold preventative with high doses of vitamin C" is now relegated to a placebo prescription. Adolescents of the mid-sixties had spread the word that the inner layer of banana skin contained a powerful psychedelic similar to LSD and reported glorious "trips" after smoking the dried scrapings. But they really tripped on their own wishes and a placebo effect. Today we have Noni.

Some years ago psychiatric journals reported severe panic reactions in people smoking cannabis for the first time. A typical case described a man in his late thirties "straight laced and square, wanting to feel freer, who decided to try a joint." After one or two puffs the panic developed, not caused by the marijuana but by fears that had built up in his mind about it. These cases are much rarer now since cannabis is more commonplace and no longer a dread, powerful substance. Nevertheless, a number of terminally ill patients have refused a medical offer of cannabis to enhance anesthetic medication because they experienced fear and guilt about using a proscribed substance even if legally obtained.

Placebo in cannabis (48)

Tetra-hydro-cannabinol (THC), the active ingredient of all varieties of the cannabis plants, was offered to experienced marijuana users in different doses of THC-saturated and THC-free cigarettes with only the flavor and scent of THC. Pure THC in measured liquid and tablet form was also given. The degree of intoxication was remarkably independent of the amount of pure THC absorbed into the body. Those results, which have yet to be refuted, demonstrated that a placebo effect influenced to a greater or lesser degree an anticipated intoxication to the test items, with or without THC. These findings contradicted the widely held belief that cannabis produced an intoxication that had specific, readily identifiable features.

A proposal has been been offered in the medical world that, because of its universal presence in therapeutics, "placebo" should be included in the concept of "drug." Research projects are studying the efficacy of "placebo" prescriptions, and attempting to isolate the mechanism of the reaction. Psychiatric News (82) stated "Placebo response can confound drug trials. Not only is there initial improvement in both drug and placebo groups in trials of psychiatric drugs, but the placebo group often improves so much that it is difficult for the drug group to achieve a significant, additional improvement. It is like testing an anti-depressant in a population that isn't depressed." Psychiatrists are now urging physicians to take the gains from placebo effects more seriously.

Common misconceptions regarding cannabis have been challenged recently from different sources. Local professors at the University of the West Indies, and researchers in the United States are questioning whether the various dangers and the fearsome imagery surrounding marijuana use in the thinking of the public are justified in reality. Researchers have become more receptive to proposals offered in 1944 by the United States' federal narcotic research facility to decriminalize cannabis and stop the demoralizing prison sentences for possession. Reactions of the public and fears of the professional sector had thwarted that proposal.

Placebo and quackery, pre-1935 (42)

Commercialization of quackery was prominent in the 1800s when ignorance and outright lying characterized folk medicine cures. The 1897 Sears, Roebuck catalogue (95) devoted dozens of pages to advertise "safe" patent medicines and home remedies for a wide variety of medical complaints. A predominant promise was the "safe" relief of "nervous tension." Chemical analysis of the "safe" remedies revealed a strong concentration of both opium and alcohol. The catalogue openly advertised laudanum, which is opium dissolved in alcohol and a much favored potion for its sedative effect with "nervous ladies of class," at six cents an ounce. Further, Sears claimed that their "White Star Liquor Cure" added to supper coffee blocked an alcoholic's interest in drinking at the neighborhood saloon. He would fall asleep at the dinner table! The cure's effective ingredient was opium. The unfortunate alcoholic who became opium-dependent as a result of the liquor cure could find "Treatment of the Morphine and Opium Habit" on other pages. The secret ingredient—alcohol!

The travelling "medical man," dispenser of nostrum cure-alls promising restoration of hair to the bald, potency to the impotent, cure of kidney and liver ills, and relief of all disabilities should not be forgotten. Today the prominent lures are the promises in pharmaceutical advertisements."Magical thinking," determines the success or failure of potions, rituals, medicine men, witch doctors, faith healers, fad diets, health pills, and much of alternative medicine.

Di-acetyl morphine. (19)

Although community compliance to quackery reflected the naivete of an uninformed citizenry in believing vendor and therapist claims, a similar situation existed in the scientific sector. Early in the 1900s di-acetyl morphine was produced and hailed enthusiastically as a "cure for morphine addiction." Di-acetyl morphine is better known as heroin. Since then it is a thrice-told tale.

Proliferation of substances

Technological advances dramatically expanded and diversified Man's monopoly as sole creator, dispenser, and user of a myriad of substances collectively called "drugs." Man's timeless wish to banish suffering and achieve pleasure always seemed near to fulfillment, and a substance that produced a comfortable frame of mind effortlessly and quickly would seem magical. People have always wanted quick and easy, "magical," satisfactions. As technology delivered the goods, and the magic potions seemed here now, appetites were whetted. In his pursuit of the magic substances Man discovered many substances with powerful effects. He learned to ferment fruit to alcohol; he discovered morphine and cocaine along with penicillin, aspirin, and digitalis. Their real chemical effects, however, only reinforced his belief in magic. These were "magic gifts from heaven," spurring him on in his unremitting search for more. Many reasoned that if some is good, more is better.

New substances, introduced yearly, are always proudly haled with fanfares of great hopes as "Wonder Drugs" which are then soon replaced by a new batch of the same. Manufacture and marketing of all therapies are "big businesses," while the new product oftimes may only be an improvement on some old side effect. The medical problem persists leading both the public and the provider to wish for "better magic." Pharmaceutical houses have publicly called a truce to their ongoing competitive race for the newest, safest, and most effective wonder drug to replace last year's products because the products became too expensive for them to produce and users to buy. More and more physicians were then forced to prescribe medications that are increasing in price at a phenomenal rate.

Magic manufactured

In the 19th century advances in technology uncovered complex chemistries which led to an over-abundance of substances with effects on mind and body. Manufacture proceeded along rational, scientific paths. But the repetitive media and medical accolades proclaiming surprise about drugs "that work like magic" suggested that the motivation for creating new drugs reflected the age-old wish for more magic substances, not primarily a need for more therapeutic agents. "Miraculous," "beyond our wildest dreams," "a panacea," "a cure all," "Demerol—at last a safe substitute for the opiates"(4) were the unrealistic, overly optimistic acclaims. Currently allegations are made that a new tranquilizer pill can alleviate symptoms of four different psychiatric conditions, if one believes the advertisement.

Merck manual

Misinformation and the absence of reliable medical data in the 19th century was underscored in the medical science document, "Merck's

Manual of Materia Medica." The "Manual" (73) was first published in 1899 by the reputable pharmaceutical firm of Merck as a giveaway 198 page reference pocketbook for physicians. One section listed every agent then thought to be of therapeutic value (absinthe as tonic, to zinc fluorinate for nervousness). Poisons were dispensed until recognized as such.Digitalis, curare, codeine, quinine, atropine are some medicaments that are still prescribed. Cannabis, opium, cocaine, paraldehyde, bromides, and chloral hydrate were used interchangeably for a wide variety of diagnoses that dated back to Galen's time. Unusual prescriptions for treatment of tetanus included alcohol, cannabis, cocaine, and chloroform; for insomnia, opium was prescribed; for meningitis, opium and strychnine were given; for prostatitis, leeches to the perineum were advised.

The second section of the handbook indexed all known illnesses, with the last section listing the treatments. A statement justifying an extraordinary number of procedures with little or no value was "it was thought better to do something than nothing"—enter placebo! Updates with new discoveries of "chemicals and drugs with therapeutic indications" corrected earlier misinformation. The Manual, now a respected medical textbook of more than 2833 pages, has been in publication longer than any other general textbook of medicine in the English language.

1912 call to arms: first opium convention

In the early 1900s politicians ignited community anxieties about "an expanding threat of narcotic addiction over the world." Political lobbying to declare war against opium led to the formation of the First Opium Convention at The Hague in 1912. Convened by the Emperor of Russia, The King of England and Emperor of India, the Kaiser of Germany, the President of France, and the President of the United

States, the convention's aim was to "bring about the gradual suppression of the abuse of opium." The earlier Opium Wars (24) of 1839-1844 and 1856-1860, were waged between Chinese and other governments' economic-political factions maneuvering for control of the lucrative monopoly of the opium trade. They were fought to ensure continuation of the poppy's lucrative market, not suppress its "abuses."

Cannabis, not mentioned in the text of the original agenda, was only introduced in The Hague conferences as an after-thought (29). During the 1912 Convention, with no scientific documentation and over strong opposition from France and England, Egypt had introduced a motion that "the conference considered it desirable to study cannabis from a statistical and scientific point of view with the object of limiting its abuses." Grown in India, brought into Central America, Mexico, and South America by the Spanish conquistadors in the 18th and 19th centuries, cannabis had not been previously judged as a fearsome social problem in the East or West Indies. Opium and cannabis, prevalent for centuries, were suddenly and inexplicably judged as "global threats to the world" (29). During the Second Conference of 1924 in Geneva under the League of Nations, continuing discussion decided cannabis should be controlled as a "narcotic," like opium.

They knew not with what they dealt

Blunder in term

"Narcotic," a pharmacological term, properly refers only to opium derivatives and certain synthetics that produce equivalent effects. Morphine, heroin, codeine, methadone, Demerol, Talwin are properly called "narcotics"; illegal cocaine, cannabis, LSD, peyote, and mescaline each with different effects, are not. Linking cannabis, opium, and cocaine under the umbrella term of "narcotic" was a terminology Babel blunder of the 1912 Convention. Apart from revealing the reformers' gross ignorance of various substances' effects, the blunder set the stage for any proscribed substance to be incorrectly thought of as a "narcotic" by the uninformed. All substances labelled "dangerous" were also "illegal" and came under the jurisdiction of the Bureau of Narcotics in the United States (106) after 1914. Illegal substances were loosely called "narcotic drugs" and users "addicts." Therefore the number of "narcotics" and "drugs," along with the "addict" census rapidly expanded without reliable scientific evidence. The terms "controlled," "dangerous and illegal drugs" unfortunately and incorrectly remain as synonyms for "narcotic" in the public's minds. Possession or sale of an "illegal" substance, not use, became the crime. Cannabis was condemned, and the Harrison Narcotic Act also added cocaine to its list of "narcotics" in 1925.

Confusion and controversy are inevitable in any consideration of the drug issue. One important source of difficulty is semantic. The arguing participants are using the same words but are defining them differently. The law can classify any substance as a problem and just as easily revoke problem status. Legal definitions of "drug problem" vary with changes in public attitudes. The medical view of drug abuse emphasizes that abuse is the use of unprescribed, unsupervised "addictive substances." Legal attitudes frequently oppose medical opinion and strange inconsistencies result. Illegal marijuana has yet to be proven dangerous or "addictive" by medical standards, alcohol is legal yet people get "addicted" to it. While legal and medical definitions are unstable and contradict each other, popular usage is stable but skewed. Everyday references to the "drug problem" conjure up overtones of danger, illegality, sexual abandon, and murderous muggings by "dope fiends." To define terms is no mere exercise in professorial hairsplitting. How can the drug problem be defined without that indispensable first step of defining "drug."

Alcohol

Not mentioned at conference cocktail parties as a social danger, alcohol escaped condemnation even though its prevalence and use far exceeded all other substances combined. Alcohol has had a whirlwind history of statutory changes from legal to illegal and back to legal. When its sale and possession were illegal under the Volstead Act in the United States, ethyl alcohol could be obtained in a pharmacy, "a drug store," on a physician's prescription. Old-fashioned alcoholism, many times more prevalent than narcotics abuse, suffers from neglect by comparison. It is even studied apart from the drug problem. Still not classified as a "drug" in the legal or lay sectors, though medically it is so labelled, alcohol and alcoholism (62) are studied apart from the "drug problem" as if they are unique. Advertisements exhort, "if you know someone with a drug or drinking problem, call—."

The latest targets for "drug abuse suppression" are cigarettes and tobacco which are now in the "drug" bag. Has it been decided that "possession or sale of tobacco or cigarettes" is a criminal activity, a social-illness symptom, a reaction to economic stress, a sign of psychiatric illness, or even a normal activity? All categories, in fact, are possible considerations! Fortunes will accrue either by attacking or defending tobacco in the anti-smoking crusades. In 1940 a burning cigarette paper was known to release an allegedly carcinogenic acid. Health officials had also pointed out that five deep breaths of New York City air filled lungs with many pathogens and carcinogens. Where does re-breathing cigarette smoke in restaurants fit in? And in the same vein, why isn't there an action against those who drive cars and trucks with oilseal leaks spewing black smoke?

Terminology Babel

Before 1900, clinical or statistical terms as elemental as "drug" or "addict" had not been scientifically defined. "What is a drug?" The answer varied with the generation in which it was asked. Inaccurate terminology created a formidable obstacle to defining "drugs," "drug problem," and "drug addict."

Dictionaries today continue an ambiguity noted in editions of the 1800s that defined "drugs" in two, diametrically opposed ways: as either a benevolent curative whose presence or use posed no social opprobrium or legal sanctions, a medicament; or conversely, as a poison or toxin whose possession or use is condemned by society. The lexicon states that the term "potion," derived from the same root word as "poison," explicitly referred to a substance that possessed magical qualities for either benevolent or evil uses.

Phrases using the term "drug" appeared in profusion. "He has a drug problem" could signify medical, legal, or social consequences from a person's use of a substance; or, a community "drug problem," could be a community's fear of the presence of and traffic in illegal substances. A substance itself might be called "a problem drug," and the desire to use it a "drug problem." Barbiturate sedatives, amphetamine diet pills, along with tranquilizers and other mood-and thought-altering substances enlarged the "drug" chest. As a consequence, even the volume of substances became a "drug problem." There was much talk about "drugs" but no agreement as to definition. Additional undefined terms such as "designer drugs, recreational drugs, hard drugs," only increased definition confusion.

In response to the alarmed public's appeal that something be done to make the world drug-free, inexperienced "drug control experts" arose over the years from the ranks of various professions and academic disciplines, even from groups of "ex-addicts." Since no scientific research in drug addiction had preceded the alarm no precise or consensus of terminology existed to orient strategies for a "War Against Drugs." The many theories offered by citizens unsophisticated in the subject represented only personal opinions. Making sense of the complex tangle of issues of individual psychopathology, professional management, legal argument, and society's many different moral reactions, beliefs, and warnings regarding use, defied the inexperienced.

To prevent the creation of another Tower of Babel theorists should have reached a consensus of scientific definition of their target before plans for controls were proposed. The questions "What are drugs? What is an addict?" should have opened the 1912 Hague Convention, but didn't. Members of the original convention signed the treaty of 1912, and along with the 1914 Harrison Narcotic Act and the Marijuana Tax Stamp Act in the United States (106), made "possession, sale, or traffic in opium or cannabis illegal unless certain license fees were paid." Note clearly, "unlicensed sale or possession," not "use," was the crime. Suspicions that financial gains via licence fees were motivating the "save the world reform" were not investigated.

Media hyperbole involved

After "War" was declared a torrent of media reports with heavy emphasis on the shocking and sensational deluged the public in the 1920s..."shooting up in the streets," "overdose fatal to teenagers," "drug addicts loose in New York" drew exaggerated images of danger in the streets from "dope-crazed junkies." The New York Times in 1921 alleged

"300,000 addicts in the United States; 30,000 addicts in New York City, each on a $50 a day habit; thousands of lives lost to narcotic overdoses." Repeated in 1927 and then again in 1950 these same allegations filled the public with the tragedies of drug addiction, the suicidal lifestyles of addicts, and the images of "drug-crazed addicts." Statistics of uncertain credibility were delivered with very little uncertainty.

Research prior to 1935

Physiological investigative research in "drug addiction" was absent throughout the 19th century. Prior to 1935, the treating physicians' personal opinions dictated treatment regimes which were restricted to the substitution of sedatives such as bromides, chloral hydrate, barbiturates, or paraldehyde for the opiate. Purges, spas, diets were considered appropriate remedies by hospital-based physicians.

"Insulin sub-coma therapy," was developed by Dr. Manfred Sakel, a psychiatrist, for the treatment of schizophrenia in the 1930s (94). He observed that a reduction in blood-sugar levels occurred during sub-coma insulin treatments in his schizophrenic morphinist patients. Sakel then used sub-coma insulin as a withdrawal procedure for opium addiction. One of many findings in the opiate abstinence syndrome is an elevation in blood sugar that would predictively be reduced with insulin, as in diabetes. The continuing and worsening of other objective signs such as vomiting, diarrhea, weight loss, fever, and sweating proved that the abstinence syndrome was running its normal course unchecked, even worsened. Sakel had incorrectly believed that by lowering the blood sugar he combatted the withdrawal illness, and so was faced with two illnesses, withdrawal illness and hypoglycemia. Based on his reports, other physicians had adopted sub-coma insulin therapy even though it led to death in many patients. It was not until 1940, after the U.S. Public Health Service Hospital at Lexington, Kentucky embarked on its studies of all detoxification procedures, that the insulin regimen, along with other touted "cures," was discredited and abandoned (111).

Psychological references: pre-1935

Psychological studies of morphinists were introduced in 1890 by a group of psychoanalysts that included Freud, Simmel, Tausk, and Rado (36,89). They drew attention to "non-addicts" (non-morphinists) who behaved with food, fetishes, love relationships, and tobacco "like morphinists with opium." Freud (34) expressed the idea that "some peculiarity in the user is necessary for an addiction to develop," and, humorously, that thumb-sucking followed by masturbation were the first "addictions." From 1935 on, however, a flood of studies in pharmacology and sociology submerged from the public view the quiet studies of the psychology of use.

Most people associate the term "psychoanalysis" only as a method or technique of treatment, not aware that the term psychoanalysis refers to three components: a method of observation; a theory of psychological development; and treatment. The treatment aspect is subject to wide, impassioned criticism by many uninformed but opinionated people. The psychoanalysts, as critical as the impassioned critics, are truly more cognizant than laymen about the needs and problems of the therapeutic component. The supply of information from the observational method, however, has definitively influenced and advanced studies in innumerable disciplines, among them being developmental psychology and childhood development. People tend to dismiss what offends them or eludes their understanding, as the discipline of psychoanalysis does, and "throw the baby out with the bath water." Psychoanalytic data has always been important. Despite its current external and even internal crises its factual contributions to many social problems over the decades remain solid.

In 1920, Dr. Sandor Rado, an eminent European psychoanalyst, emphasized that general psychiatry resisted psychological causations (87). "Clinical psychiatry," he wrote, "regards the disorders known as alcoholism and morphinism, or as an inclusive designation drug addiction, as caused by somatic toxins. They are classified as 'mental disorders of exogenous (outside the body) origin'. From this point of view the process of mental dilapidation presented in the clinical picture of addiction would appear to be the mental manifestations of injury to the brain produced by the poisons. The investigation of the addictions has imposed on it by this idea, as its first task, the determination of the cerebral effects of the noxious substances on the brain. Its goal would be an exact correlation of the course of the disorder with the toxic processes in the brain. The problem includes not only direct toxic influences on the brain, but also indirect influences by toxic products from other affected organs in the body. It is consequently not remarkable that the somatic causation hypothesis of addiction has borne so little fruit." Rado's statement, "not the toxic agent but the impulse to use it makes the addict," challenged the various opinions and theories of use then in vogue (88,89).

The theoretical background to the strategies of the "War" retained the unsupported "somatic toxin" theory of addiction. Psychiatry held fast to this theory through the 1970s because the medical model of infection and disease was familiar to a physician. To be sure, the fact that alcohol does not cause alcoholism the way a pneumococcus causes pneumonia was not ignored. A bacterium attacks a person regardless of what the victim's wishes may be. The drinker, however, attacks his own body voluntarily by his own wish to take in the toxin. How or why substances entered the body at the start of addiction oddly was not studied by the researchers. Neglect of such questions reflected close-mindedness to psychological factors. The "drug problem" studies should have integrated human motivations in the "birth" of drugs into them. But hypotheses that projected human psychology into the "epidemic" were dismissed out of hand or ridiculed.

Ill-conceived programs and recommendations derived from misinformation, undocumented opinions, and the flawed somatic-toxin theoretical underpinning led to the unproductive strategies of "preach, prohibit; form posses; put addicts on a desert island in the Pacific like lepers; treat a sick society; give them all the drugs they want." Unworkable programs presented to an apprehensive, misinformed public crushed their hopes that had been raised for "drug problem cures in a drug-free world" (97,100).

Costs of programs escalated yearly wasting enormous sums of money. From 1981 to 1990 in the United States alone, $150 billion tax dollars were spent on "drug problem" projects. 93 percent went to "law enforcement" and other budgets, but only 7 percent for clinical research of users. This expenditure was repeated by the end of 1997, while the United States continued urging or coercing other countries to join the war (106).

Inaccuracies of terminology and theory clearly existed in the strategies of "cure" at their inception. The mix of flawed theory, undefined terms, clinical inexperience, absence of scientifically obtained data, widespread emotionalism in regard effects of use, particularly cannabis, irrational theorizing, ordained failure about measures "to make the world drug free." Since an informed consensus had not been reached about what the "drug abuse problem" was, no rational plans could have been formulated to solve it. Certainly "War" could not be fought using flawed strategies.

Mandate for research: enter Narco

Such was the state of ignorance, ambiguity, and confusion about "drugs and addiction" prior to 1935. The need for objective, scientific information led the United States in 1935 to mandate research into "the little understood topic of narcotic addiction." The U.S. Public Health Hospital at Lexington, Kentucky, nick named Narco, became the venue.

A federal prison hospital, Narco admitted two types of patients: voluntary patients seeking to either detoxify, or "to give up an opiate habit" were the first type. Detoxification, by reducing their current high levels of daily intake, would allow patients to leave the hospital needing, for a short while, less of their expensive opiate. The second type were either convicted prisoners or parole violators returned to complete sentences for opium or cannabis possession. As knowledge of Lexington's existence spread (26), users of other types of substances, such as barbiturates, amphetamines, and Demerol sought voluntary admission. A demographic profile of the hospital census revealed a cross-section of any metropolitan city with all economic, educational, ethnic, and sociological sectors represented (79).

Narco's clinical research from 1936, winning world-wide recognition, covered a broad field. The investigations marked the dawn of modern scientific study of drug abuse that would correct many conceptual errors of the past and add new, objective, scientific, diagnostic data. Medical, psychiatric, psychological, and sociological studies of morphinists were begun (40,41). Research in animal physiology, neuropharmacology, pharmacology, and biochemistry added to the depth of the studies carried out for the first time under one roof. An accurate picture of the natural course of physical dependence, definitions of phenomena, formulations of "drug" terminology, methods of detoxification, rehabilitative programs, and an incomplete hypothesis of "drug addiction" evolved.

Dawn of research 1935

Time and space limitations allow only a sampling of the studies from the volumes of Narco's contributions (57,58) to "drug addiction." Relevance to drug theory formation will be the focus of my choice.

Volunteer patients entering off the streets and prisoner patients who had been in custody for weeks showed no objective signs of abstinence syndromes. Since no definitive studies of the abstinence syndrome existed, Narco, therefore, decided to give first priority to produce the syndrome. Prisoners who agreed to participate in a clinical study volunteered to receive measured doses of morphine sulfate four times a day for a month which was to be then abruptly discontinued. Physical dependence, which had developed over the month, then released a "cold turkey" reaction, an abstinence syndrome. The many signs of morphine abstinence could be observed and quantified. This precise method of data gathering probably could not be used in the year 2001 needing, as it does, a prison hospital as its venue with trained researchers and personnel. Leaning heavily on the empirical physiological data of the morphine abstinence syndrome, Narco established criteria to define "addict, addicted, and addictive substance" (58).

Narco's definitions

"Addicted," an ambiguous term, was replaced with the designation "physical dependency," a biochemical state that occurs in body cells after prolonged administration of any, and probably all, substances. The changes are of such a nature that when intake of that substance is stopped in a person physically dependent on it, a characteristic abstinence syndrome for that substance may appear.

Opiates produce physical dependence and tolerance in one month, escalating from starting doses of fifteen milligrams taken four times a day to thirty milligrams four times daily. Abrupt stoppage, leads to gooseflesh, from which the term "cold turkey" withdrawal is derived. Profuse perspiration, and complaints of chills and muscle pain worsen when joined by nausea, vomiting, diarrhea, and fever causing a sizable loss of weight from dehydration. The presence of an opiate physical dependence is confirmed when its abstinence syndrome develops within 36 hours after the last dose of morphine. The syndrome runs a diminishing course of intensity for five to seven days (56) but can be stopped with a therapeutic dose of morphine. The morphine "abstinence syndrome" became the paradigm of physical dependence studies because its clearly observable signs, which are the consequences not the initial causes of use, were useful as basic criteria,

Prior to 1935, the term "addict" specified an opiate habitue, but later was extended to users of other substances. The condition of "being an addict," a psychological state, required evidence that habituation or psychological dependence, and loss of control over a drug use in daily life existed. By relapsing after repeated detoxifications a morphine habitue demonstrated that psychological dependence was present and he would be diagnosed as "an addict."

"Ex-addict" could not be defined because the cause of use wasn't identified. Since frequent relapses to use, even after many years "drug free," could be expected, discharged patients should never be called "cured," only "drug free." A detoxified patient, mislabelled as an "ex-addict," should not be sent out to the public as an expert to claim the virtues of some procedure. "Medical addict" is an incorrect, widely misused term to describe a patient who required morphine for a period of time in sufficient amount for him/her to become physically dependent during a medical illness. After detoxification when the medical reason subsided, such a patient did not continue to use morphine independently. These are examples of misuse of terms showing how inaccurate definitions from invalid theoretical concepts give rise to false diagnoses.

Tolerance refers to the decreasing response of the body to a current dosage and usually accompanies the development of physical dependence. To maintain an effective blood concentration and prevent the occurrence of abstinence signs in a person physically dependent, dosage must be periodically increased. Physical dependence and tolerance are then both escalated in a vicious circle that morphinists call "hooked."

The terms "addicted" and "addict," though clearly defined, left difficulties with other terms. The term an "addictive drug" is commonly used to designate substances that are claimed to produce or not to produce physical dependence, tolerance, and psychological dependence. "Addictive drug," would warn the user that the substance was "dangerous and legally controlled"; non-addictive therefore meant "safe to be used," as Demerol had been classed at first. A meaningless term used primarily by pharmaceutical firms for marketing promotions, "addictive" is an active-tense word. It carries the misleading implication that the drug produces the psychological state of addiction and that physical dependence is the cause not a consequence of use. Various media, especially medical journals carrying pharmaceutical advertisements, show wishful thinking in their inflated promises that serve the financial profit of pharmaceutical houses. Demerol when it first appeared was claimed to be "non-addicting except for people who had been previously addicted to morphine" (4). Three years later in 1946 an advance guard of Demerol users who had never used morphine sought detoxification (110). The obvious had been ignored: if a substance produced a certain wished-for effect, some people would continue to self-medicate, or "abuse" a substance, on their own. There are no safe drugs.

Differentiation of terms

Narco precisely differentiated the terms "physical dependence" and "abstinence syndrome" from each other. These terms for different but closely related physiological conditions had been widely misused as synonyms for "addiction," a complex psychological state, or "habit." Using the term "physical dependence" as a synonym for "addiction," the media coined the misleading and certainly lurid terms "baby addicts" and "monkey addicts." Opiates taken regularly by a pregnant woman will produce physical dependence in her unborn child. An abstinence syndrome will appear in the baby when its birth prevents the forced, involuntary intake, or if the pregnant mother stops her own intake. The primates from Southeast Asia do not greedily ingest the opium poppy growing in profusion there, but require isolation in cages to be forcibly injected to develop physical dependence. Detoxification of the baby or monkey removes physical dependence, not "addiction." The "forced intake" of morphine imposed on the babies or monkeys is diametrically opposite to "compulsive voluntary intake" of morphinists, a difference overlooked in the sensationalism of media mis-information.

Other syndromes

Abstinence syndromes for different substances, such as alcohol, Demerol, barbiturates, amphetamines were studied and quantified (46,50,55,111). Other substances such as peyote, mescaline, LSD-25 (55) did not fulfill the diagnostic criteria as set down by the USPHS but were kept on the list of "addictive," "narcotic," "dangerous" and illegal drugs of the Bureau of Narcotics.

Before the barbiturate abstinence syndrome was recognized, a number of fatalities occurred during opiate withdrawal. Morphinists commonly supplemented their expensive opiates with cheap, easy to obtain sedatives and tranquilizers. If physical dependence had developed to these supplements, an abrupt and unwitting stoppage of their intake could lead to convulsions, psychosis, or death (50). The alcohol abstinence syndrome which develops two days after abrupt withdrawal is characterized by tremors, delirium, and hallucinations, the infamous "D.T.'s." Severe dehydration which develops becomes life threatening.

Governed by the rate and amount consumed, alcohol and cannabis can produce similar ranges of intensities of intoxications and therefore they appeal to a large population of users. Their similar intoxicant range has led to the replacing of alcohol with cannabis in religious communities proscribing alcohol, as in Islam. Hashish, from which the term assassin was derived, was smoked before battle allegedly to make Islamic warriors more fierce, just as non-Islamic soldiers might use alcohol. However, individual reactions with either substance varied and were not predictively "murderous." Japanese kamikaze pilots reduced their fears more successfully with high doses of amphetamines that stimulated impulsivity.

Cannabis

No detoxification procedures were needed for cannabis (55) or cocaine since no abstinence syndromes, no physical dependence, could be demonstrated in abstinence studies. Most prisoner cannabis-users had not used opium even casually and demonstrated none of the new diagnostic criteria of "addict" (55). In 1944 Narco argued for its decriminalization. The scientific community lost this argument to political expediency, emotionalism of the uninformed reacting to mistaken opinions, and the need of the Bureau of Narcotics to protect its expanding bureaucracy.

Under legal restraints, cannabis reproduced the history of alcohol when the latter was controlled by the Volstead Act. Marijuana suppliers and the old-fashioned "bootleggers and gangsters" are mirror images. With the Volstead Act's repeal, bootleggers became wealthy business people and productive citizens. Holland relaxed its restrictions of marijuana usage in 1976, as Narco had recommended in 1944. Current debates are now repeating arguments for and against "legalizing or decriminalizing cannabis."

Methadone (45)

Germany synthesized methadone in the late 1930's during World War II when Turkey cut off Germany's supplies of medically needed morphine. Originally called Dolophine in honor of Adolph Hitler, renamed 10820 and then amidone, the drug was liberated in 1940 as "methadon" to Narco's research staff for investigation. Narco evaluated methadon, which picked up an "e" to become "methadone," as a superb narcotic, capable of achieving everything morphine or heroin did, perhaps better. Meeting all medical and pharmacological criteria established by Narco, methadone was recommended for regulation as a narcotic under the Harrison Narcotic Act. "Would it become abused like opiates?" was an anxious question. A flat, emphatic "Yes" was the answer. Confirmation of the prediction of abuse came in due course as the census of methadone dependent people grew.

Narco proved that opiates and methadone are cross tolerant (46), meaning they possess equivalent pharmacological reactions that permit interchangeability. Methadone produces physical dependence and tolerance in one month escalating from an initial dose of five to ten milligrams four times per day to thirty milligrams four times per day.An abstinence syndrome appears three days after abrupt stoppage; opiate abstinence appears in twelve hours. The methadone abstinence syndrome peaks between the fifth and ninth day subsiding between day ten and twelve. Opium's "cold turkey" peaks in thirty-six hours and subsides in seven days. Methadone remains in the body longer, accounting for its abstinence signs to appear later, and for these signs to last longer. Further, methadone abstinence illness is subjectively less severe than the opiate.

Because of their interchangeability, clinical trials of methadone for detoxification of opiate-dependent voluntary patients were begun. Substitution regimes investigated on my admission-withdrawal service in 1947 proved methadone suppressed and eliminated the opiate abstinence syndrome. This result was also a boon for cancer patients requiring narcotics for long periods to control agonizing bone pain. Tolerance to morphine would build up to dangerously high dosages that now could be comfortably reduced or discontinued by substituting methadone until the tolerance to morphine diminished. Therefore, by alternating them at low doses, physical dependence and tolerance to either narcotic could be kept at manageable levels.

Because it is accompanied by emotional stress that can lead to suicide, drug withdrawal or detoxification should only be attempted in a special hospital setting. Additionally, no treatment for a physical dependence should be initiated before its presence is confirmed by a short period of "cold turkey." Otherwise treatment may be given when not needed. Narco advised ten-day gradual detoxification withdrawal procedures to both monitor and avoid the cruel and dangerous full blown "cold turkey" (58).

People had irrationally blamed the substances that they had created pre-1935 and in later years, for their being used, for their adverse social consequences, and for "personal problems they caused." Linguistically man depicted himself as a passive victim of drugs; "demon rum" captured him; morphine enslaved him. Drugs were active, "dangerous," they "took people." By 1940, the desperate crusade that had begun in the early 1900s to make the "world drug free," was intensified. Self-defeating, however, because production and diversification were simultaneously increased. As Walt Kelly's "Pogo" would say, "We have met the enemy and he is us!"

Activities at Narco

Not only involved with clinical research data, Narco had also tried to develope and support rehabilitative programs considered innovative in their day. Six months of hospitalization were arbitrarily proposed as the "healing" time needed for mind and body; Halfway houses were endorsed as aids to social re-entry; individual and group psychotherapy were encouraged. The first chapter of Narcotics Anonymous, a spinoff from Alcoholics Anonymous and forerunner to Synanon and other self-help groups, was started and supported at Narco; day-care centers staffed by "ex-addicts" were abandoned after abuses and incompetence were revealed.

Rehabilitation projects, professional public education campaigns, and changes in drug laws were proposed with the endorsement of the USPHS. The state of Kentucky enacted a statute, the "Bluegrass Law," enabling opium and marijuana law violators to avoid criminal prosecution by voluntarily hospitalizing themselves at Narco for six months, or until discharged by the hospital. The law failed to achieve its purpose of helping abusers and was discontinued. Apparently disregarding, or unaware of, Kentucky's failed "Bluegrass Law," New York State tried a similar failed approach in 1950. Not to be outdone, Florida also enacted a clone.

Psychiatric News of September 15th, 2000 reported on a project in New York State, started after a glowing report of a "Drug Court" project in Florida that had begun in 1989. As a panacea to the overwhelming number of drug related cases clogging the New York court systems, judicial reforms would launch court-mandated substance abuse treatment and provide nonviolent drug-addict offenders with an important choice. They would have the option of going to statewide treatment facilities instead of jail. The screening of those nonviolent user began, but how decisions were reached was not clear.

It would seem history repeated itself with a plan that had failed in Kentucky in the 1950s. Also the program fails to consider that no advances in treatment procedures have been reported, and the training and supervision of the people in charge is not mentioned. The intent is noteworthy but is doomed to fail as others before it have.

School programs for educating about dangers of drug abuse did not and do not fulfill their aim of curtailing use. Public over-confidence in educational campaigns and advertising gimmicks to erase the consequences of inadequate child-rearing practices in the homes of rich and poor, or to undo psychological damage from pathological experiences was never justified. The expectation that warnings on cigarette packs or in bars would deter the use of tobacco or alcohol grossly underrated the strength of the psychological forces propelling their use and youths' readiness to resist any suppression of their impulses. Adults' prohibitions are usually taken as "dares" by children and teenagers to be challenged and acted upon.A misinformed philosophy to prevent use assumes that if "you scare the hell out of kids, by showing the sordid life styles of addicts to school children then they won't touch it." That doesn't work.

Repeatedly over the years various agencies and community groups resurrected failed programs that had been abandoned. Overly optimistic, unrealistic proposals in the 1970s and 1980s supported by authoritative sources, such as NIDA (National Institute on Drug Abuse), went unchallenged and become accepted strategies. Unsound hypotheses of the past not re-evaluated by the new crop of experts initiated a monotonous parade of the past failures under the guise of new and innovative. However, even the revival of ineffectual programs, about which the average citizen knew nothing, allowed the equally unknowledgeable self-appointed expert-politician, to falsely reassure the public, "We are doing something. Programs are in place!"

Flaw in theory

Despite important contributions, Narco could not derive a consensus-agreed definition of "drug" or theory of "drug addiction." The prestige of the USPHS and their research, as well as that of the National Institute of Drug Abuse and the American Psychiatric Association, had allowed the flawed somatic theory underpinning to dominate unchallenged the research environs. Under emphasis of psychological factors obstructed derivation of a valid theory. Dr. Harris Isbell, chief of research at Narco, said in 1951, "There is already a great body of pharmacological and physiological information, but too little psychological." Other researchers stated in 1974 that their experiences paralleled Isbell's. "There have been no treatment (or research) programs which focus on the massive character pathology, the severe neurotic, and the relatively frequent psychotic states impelling abuse" (113,120). Until 1965, international governments' acceptance of a theory of "psychological causation" of drug use was rejected for the more palatable lip-service acknowledgment of "psychological problems as consequences of use." This stubbornly defended flaw in concept, confusing "cause" with "consequence," continues to mislead investigators.

"The anti-psychological bias of many scientists and psychiatrists was almost a psycho-phobia, or a deep-seated fear of taking emotional life seriously. Psychological factors were diluted by being tightly interwoven with legal, economic, and political factors with their moral values of power, expediency, success, and cost efficiency spawning strategies of manipulation that were to pass as programs of therapy" (120). By 1940 politics and legalisms of drug use had entered the game of theorizing on the drug scene. The United States, by supplying advisers, funds, and itself as a role model bragged about its "sound" programs even as its law and order thrusts of stiff laws and punishment of addicts proved to be complete failures. Government experts of political policy-making were not experts in producing policies of substance control. Unable to differentiate "drug use" from "drug smuggling," which are tangentially related but structurally different situations, planners increased anti-smuggling laws as the way to "cure" the world's drug abuse—a mass cure for which there is no known specific disease!

Coercion of other countries to follow its lead in expanding anti-drug abuse campaigns, a euphemism for "law and order," is still maintained by the United States. Their unsuccessful programs led to a mushrooming of enforcement needs of more men, money, and laws. Clinton wanted to expand the police anti-smuggling approach and continue that failed program. The Reagan war on drug-abuse had been criticized by members of Congress who wondered how much of the highly publicized Reagan concern had been simple rhetoric of political expediency.

In 1977 William Pollin, M.D. Director of Research at the National Institute on Drug Abuse, prefaced a United States government monograph "First Technical Review of the Psychodynamics of Drug Dependence" (71) with, "over the past two decades research in drug dependence focused primarily on pharmacokinetics, and biochemical structure.. Missing has been an equivalent emphasis at the level of the individual person, focussed on the structure and dynamics of the total personality. The papers in this monograph are a pioneering effort to discover the part played by a person's psychodynamics." Pollin thereby confirmed that the assumptions in theories about "drug abuse" focused only on the chemistry of the substances as the cause of abuse and avoided the motivations and psychology of the user. This inaccurate, biased, stance has remained in the concept of drug theory for many researchers.

Narco's physiological research was weakened by the absence of a sophisticated psychological orientation; the limited number of psycho-analytic studies (94) suffered from the absence of the extensive, objective physiological findings, the "hands on" clinical experiences, offered by Narco. Needed was the blending of expertise of the two observational methods.

Preconceptions contribute flaws

Depending on the user's wish and motive, alcohol and cannabis can produce intoxications ranging from a mild, controlled "elation" through "uncontrolled drunk" or "stoned," or release aggressive agitation, or stupor or coma; LSD creates a psychotic "trip"; opiates produce the "nod"; cocaine, amphetamines, methedrine and other stimulants lead to "speeding"; cocaine mixed with an opiate "makes one go fast slowly." One "high" does not suit all, not everyone desires the same type of "high." To want to get "high" simply means "wanting to feel good." These observations raised the question, "Why is one intoxication preferred over others?" And that question became central to a general theory of drug use.

Drug of choice, regression, intoxication

What is "intoxication"? A common but incomplete answer would state "intoxication is a behavioral change in a person's usual clear or sober state of mind resulting from the action of some substance that entered the body. By looking more closely at a number of people "intoxicated" on various substances different types of reactions will be noted. Clinical observations confirm that a user will call the quiet lethargy produced by morphine a "high"; another person will call the disorientation or stupor on barbiturates a "high"; some get high on downers or tranquilizers; others get drunk or "high" on alcohol; or a person may want just a heightened joviality as with low dose cannabis or alcohol and will call it "getting high"; another person may want to become agitated, a "high" of hyperactivity, as with cocaine or amphetamines.

Then what is "high"? The resistance of drug-program planners to accept new, objective clinical findings had created two popular false impressions that had adversely influenced all theories and decisions. One was the forceful preconceived opinion that drug abusers will promiscuously use any and all substances equally; the other, created by the incorrect belief of promiscuous use, was that the universal motive to want to use any and all intoxicants was "just wanting to get high" for pleasure.

Many substances can intoxicate or release a person from a sober state. But leaving the sober state is only half the story of intoxication; where one arrives is the other. When the total intoxication experience satisfies the user as no prior substance, experience, or relationship had done before, a preference for that particular agent develops as a "drug of choice." What had looked like promiscuous use of all drugs was a search through trials of many intoxicants to find one giving that special intoxication.

The apparent "promiscuous use" is actually a discriminating search through the testing of many and various substances(112) to satisfy a wish to "feel good." Simply put, wanting to get high is the wish to change one's frame of mind to "feel good" from "feeling bad." Despite evidence that it is not the "stepping stone to" but an unsuccessful step in the search for a special intoxication, people still voice a skewed claim that marijuana is the stepping stone to heroin. If cannabis had supplied the desired effect the search would have stopped there as it does for most people. One could just as erroneously say "alcohol is the stepping stone to opium."

Drug effects

Many of the various intoxicated states reproduce specific behavior and mental functioning characteristic of earlier phases of early childhood. All intoxications, from whatever source, are in fact regressed states. The two terms are interchangeable and synonymous as recognizable alterations in consciousness and behavior. The psychedelic LSD produces a mental disorganization so chaotic it has been called a model psychosis that youth call "blowing the mind." The mind's filtering mechanisms that normally control and process stimuli from all parts of the body are disabled. This leads to an assault on the mind by a torrent of sensory inputs. Thinking is deranged, hallucinations, and delusions appear; the fundamental difference of inside and outside the self disappears; you and me, self and non-self merge with the walls, or inanimate objects as all personal identity is lost. The "LSD trip" (intoxication) is a regression to a bewildering but not new mental state.

Its features resemble the earliest days of mental functioning during the first months of life, known as the autistic stage. Some people react with anxiety to this intoxication and will avoid further exposure, while others seek to repeat the experience. A sober, verbal, comforting companion akin to a loving parent is a necessary participant on the "trip." Unfortunately, many do not return from the regression and remain psychotic.

When a morphinist is intoxicated, he is in a passive state of mind not interested in sex, fighting, or food; and when sober or abstinent he is too sick or weak to do all the raping and killing of which he is accused. "Being on the nod," which is what users call the narcotic intoxication, resembles an early childhood defense against anxiety. Appearing between ten and fourteen months of age after a dependent tie to the mother has been established, the child may experience loneliness and fear occasioned by even momentary or brief separations from her. In a fantasy wherein all wishes and needs are satisfied, the child re-creates the previous state of union with the absent mother. Wish-fullfilling fantasies during an opium intoxication re-create the illusion of complete satiation of all needs by the yearned-for mother.

New definitions for "drug," "drug use," "drug user"

After psychological factors were upgraded and tentatively integrated with physiological research findings, changes in concepts and theory appeared. From 1950 on, an expanded definition of "drug" broadened the meaning of "drug use" and "drug user." The definition incorporated the fact of placebo stating that a "drug" may be a substance, but it need not be. Anything consistently used and sought by a person to change an undesired state of mind or body to a desired one is a "drug" for that person. This realistic expanded definition conforms to human psychology. By itself the term "use" simply means "behavior." "Drug use" is then "behavior with drugs" but does not simultaneously signify "pathological behavior." The term "drug user" may be applied to all people, from the normal "who must have coffee to start the day," through psychotic categories. The terms "drug user or drug" therefore could then be judged as being independent of the legalities, the social and personal consequences of use, and methods of acquiring the sustances that apply to the traditional concept.

The spectrum of users (50)

"Drug users" exhibit degrees of urgency of use ranging along a spec-trum from normal, occasional and under control; through transitory, moderately more intense but still under control; to more urgent, and episodically more difficult to control, as in abusive use; to consistently abusive, uncontrollable, severe compulsive addiction use. Addiction behavior is motivated by an uncontrollable, intense wish called a "crav-ing" to create as often and for as long as possible a particular state of mind, or level of consciousness. The term commonly implies a "craving for a drug," but more accurately it is a "craving for a particular mental state."

Users, arbitrarily classified into three main groups labelled Types 1, 2, and 3, are differentiated both by behavioral characteristics and the intoxications they seek. A normal person, a Type 1, may use alcohol occasionally in a social setting to add more pleasure to an already "good mood." Type 1 tries not to exceed a self-permitted temporary reduction of the usual sober state restraints. If the degree of regression is exceeded remorse may be felt when sobriety returns. The same Type 1 may tem-porarily turn into a Type 2 when an emotional stress interferes with performance of daily tasks. Normal people also experience occasional "bad times" with insomnia, anxiety, or depression, and might try a few drinks at night to sleep to permit coping with the next day's tasks. Transient Type 2 will revert spontaneously to Type 1 when the emo-tional distress passes.

A chronic Type 2 feels a persistent need to cope because of a more constant troubled sober state of mind. Urgent Type 2s blend along the spectrum into Type 3s who use alcohol compulsively not for pleasure, not to temporarily cope, but to escape from all distress. The unabating craving is to completely alter awareness of inner and outer reality. Chronic Type 2s and 3's do not use alcohol to enhance a "good time" but to escape a "bad emotional time" they cannot relieve unaided. They are not seeking "highs" or "kicks" as the uninformed believe. If a person admits, as most Type 3s do, that he/she "feels normal" only when intoxicated, then the turmoil of their sober state may be surmised. Detoxification, "drug free," lays bare the raw nerves of that sober state, the propellant of compulsive use. Compulsive opiate users call their first exposure to their drug a "joy pop," and feel "normal" which they call "straight." Objectively they are nauseated, vomiting, dizzy, their skin is intensely itchy. Mentally, however, even with the drug-induced discomfort they find relief and "normality." (50)

To repeat, a "drug" may be anything that a person believes can change an undesired state of mind or body to a desired one. The craving to re-experience a particular intoxication, or regression, becomes consciously linked to a known drug's matching effect. The type of regression-intoxication sought and the matching drug effect are the common factors linking the user and drug. The "drug of choice" could be a narcotic, or alcohol, or tranquilizer, or diets, magic rituals, over-the-counter substances, or whatever works for that person.

An understanding of the psychological mechanism known as regression, which is the revival of outgrown earlier patterns of thinking, feeling, and behaving, is the key to understanding "drug of choice." Regressions are welcomed by many emotionally troubled people because they re-establish an emotional equilibrium experienced in early childhood. The tendency to regress, which is at its most labile in childhood, diminishes in the growth to maturity. The anxieties of stress and illness, conflicted relationships in life, economic threats, inept parenting, physical trauma, even normal tasks accompanying growth and development may activate the tendency at any time of life.

The normal, transient, often dramatic regressions of children and adolescents serve important psychological needs. As temporary retreats from painful conflicts, they allow mental energies to re-accumulate before the world is faced again. Healthy adults also regress to ease the abrasions of reality but in a manner different from children. Hobbies, vacations, parties, sports, rituals, all provide avenues of retreat. After all, recreation is re-creation. "Let's have a drink or smoke" have also become common invitations at parties.

Whether the regression is "sought or fought," how much of the total personality is involved, what initiated the episode, and how long the reaction lasts are important in diagnostically assessing mental health. The depth or form of a normal or abnormal regression is pre-determined by psychological fixation points incurred during mental development from babyhood.

Under ordinary conditions "normal," Type 1 people, have safeguards, such as moral values, ethics, conscience that oppose regression and are expressed in the desire to be mature, independent, and in control of one's self. Many people, even with medically caused pain, refuse medical relief rather than feel helpless or mentally clouded by a chemically produced regression. The safeguards oppose the relinquishment of mature development and make prolonged or chaotic intoxicated states, regressive experiences, anathema to them. Regression causes a normal person to feel "not normal, not myself," and to wish for a return to their customary state of mind.

The relative freedom from chronic mental suffering in Type 1s decreases their need for escape. Types 2 and 3 have greater readiness and desire to regress since persistent troubled states generate stronger desires to escape that meet weaker opposition from the internal safeguards under attack. Controllable in Type 1, and to some extent in moderate Type 2, the need to regress in 3's and 4's becomes an urgent, uncontrollable need to escape their sober states of minds. These people do not want to experience their "normal" self, which is another way to say "I want to alter my sober state of mind." Types 1 and mild Types 2 have the capability to control their degrees of intoxication or regression, whereas severe Types 2 and 3, have little or no capability.

"Recent clinical observations of drug-dependent individuals suggest they are predisposed to addiction because they suffer with painful affect states and related psychiatric disorders. The drugs that addicts select are not randomly chosen. A 'drug of choice' results from of an interaction between a psycho-pharmacologic action of the substance and the dominant painful feeling with which they struggle.Popular or simplistic formulations in the early 1970's emphasized peer pressure, escape, euphoria, or self-destructive themes to explain the compelling nature of drug dependency. In contrast, the work of a number of psychoanalysts in the 1960s and 1970s led to observations, theoretical formulations, and subsequent studies that represented important advances and elaborations of trends set in motion in the 1950s. Developments in psychological theory enabled an appreciation that individuals will select different drugs on the basis of personality development and impairments. Their emphasis developmental considerations, adaptation, and the use of drugs as a "prosthetic" set the work of Wieder and Kaplan apart from the earlier simplistic formulations based on id, or pleasure-seeking psychology" (53).

Many compulsive users employ substances or rituals not usually considered "drugs" by the public. Obese people think constantly about food, eat without restraint even when not hungry. Some people carry water with them at all times and drink frequently, even when not thirsty. Obviously, if people eat compulsively, not out of hunger, or drink water out of compulsion not thirst, these behavior patterns would establish food or water as "drugs." Some people distort the realistic pleasure of productive work into a transient overwork to cope with a conflict at home, in a Type 2 manner, or appear as the compulsive Type 3 "workaholic" shutting out reality and all relationships behind work. Recent studies report that meditation may be used as a pleasure, coping, or escape practice. Some Type 3 meditators do not want to leave their "escape state." Compulsive gambling is another example of Type 3 behavior.

The recognition of a larger and more diversified population of drug-users embracing us all had been over-looked in the narrow view that a "drug" must have certain properties, legalisms, or social condemnation. A look at the diet market spotlights the wish, search for, and manufacture of the magic, quick pill for painless diet control and cure of obesity. Of course, the severity of legal, physiological, and psychological consequences to the user vary considerably if cocaine abuse, for example, is compared to laxative or diet pill abuse. Consequences, "problems from use," certainly may be significant, serious personal disablements, but these should not be confused with causal problems which are of an entirely different nature. Public relations techniques, however, can and do overstress the obvious difference of consequences while minimizing the strength of the compulsion for use.

Once psychological causes for drug presence and use are acknowledged as the beginning, theories and definitions of the "problem" shift from the substances to Man and his wishes. The causal compulsion may lead to food, overeating, obesity, and ill-health; or to alcohol and "skid row"; or to tranquilizers and death; or to barbiturates and psychosis; or to tobacco, water, work, meditation, coffee, or to any other "drug." To understand drug use we must look into the mind. Rado's statement, "not the toxic agent but the impulse to use it makes an addict of a person," should not be forgotten.

Treatment and control approaches

T.S. Eliot wrote, "Restoration of health is only the incubation of another malady." Freud drew attention to the fact that for many people some expression of hopefulness in the progress of their treatment makes them worse. He wrote, "Something in these people sets itself against recovery and its approach is dreaded as though it were a danger." He was among the first to warn therapists against excessive belief in the effectiveness of any specific therapy, including analysis, and against excessive zeal in imposing demands for health in the face of a patient's inability to fulfill them. In essence, to respect the need, function, and palliative nature of any symptom important to any patient's precarious stability even if society condemns the expression.

Many abusers fall into diagnostic categories of severe neuroses, borderline states, and psychoses (79,120) and may be endangered by programs introduced to help them. If thrown into a "drunk tank to dry out," or a prison cell to "kick cold turkey" unattended, patients die. Deprived of the emotional protection offered by trained hospital staff, a detoxified abuser has only three options: relapse, which can save his/her life; psychosis; or suicide. Many incarcerated compulsive abusers are found hanging in their cells. Patients can remain free of narcotics for long periods during hospitalization in a safe environment. However, often on the day of release they relapse as soon as they hit the street.

Blindly, governments responded to irrational public demands for "therapy and rehabilitation for users." What is therapy and rehabilitation? Are they something given like medicine or punishment that a patient must take? Therapy should be a non-judgmental method of aiding someone who wants help that leads to successful re-entry into the community, as rehabilitated. Governments' promises to supply therapy falsely imply that means exist or are available. Statements from the American Psychiatric Association that drug use is a "chronic, relapsing compulsion, a disease treatable by a multidisciplined approach," expresses wishful thinking of the somatic theory of abuse advocates. Who has demonstrated that such an approach brings "success" and who evaluates "success"? Who coordinates and evaluates data from diverse data, and then budgets expenditures? Studies (74) report no successes of programs based on somatic causation theories. Whether help is or is not available, 2% to 3% of compulsive users "burn out" by their middle age. Any "treatment" approach can therefore show a 2% or 3% cure rate.

It was axiomatic years ago to limit medications in psychotherapy, because the "power of a pill" would destroy the patient's trust that his psychological insights alone could achieve relief. Nowadays psychotropic medications are being prescribed for the young and the old and all types of psychiatric and medical disabilities. This presciption for health is also insisted upon by insurance companies covering the costs of treatments. How to differentiate "drug abuse of patients" from "drug abuse by patients" may be difficult. Man still believes magic resides in potions and pills to do for him what he feels unable to do for himself. And so the age-old concept that magic with capabilities to fulfill wishes resides in drugs is still with us. Established psychiatric treatment modalities are diverse, and no more special for drug-using patients than for other psychological disturbances. All therapies have inherent limitations imposed by the underlying illness of the patient and the talent of the therapist.

Maintenance therapy

Maintenance therapy is not a new or modern strategy and bears an uncanny resemblance to that which requires treatment, thereby being indistinguishable from drug abuse. In the 1920s, the United States had established clinics legally dispensing both morphine and heroin to addicts under the assumption that elimination of prosecution for illegal possession would allow addicts a "normal" life-style. All clinics closed within a few years plagued by abuses that actually continued the "addicts's" social and legal problems.

For decades a casual British system, introduced in 1950 and abolished in 1968, had permitted British physicians freedom to freely dispense narcotics in their practices. Patients, however, would obtain more than they needed and sold what they didn't use. Hoping to provide more supervision, England established free heroin-maintenance clinics for registered addicts. The British Journal of Addiction concluded that "heroin maintenance for large groups of addicts presents insoluble problems. The more they get, the more they need as the body builds up tolerance. If they get too much they can die of an overdose, but too little drives them to the illicit market."

After the opiate maintenance regimes were discontinued methadone was substituted. When community frustration boiled at the failure of methadone-maintenance programs (74), "heroin maintenance" touted as an "effective approach to drug addiction" was resurrected. In 1990 Dutch investigators, disregarding both history and Narco's scientific contributions about physical dependence and tolerance, initiated a "new treatment of opiate addiction, called heroin maintenance" thereby repeating a predictable failure. They ignored that physical dependence and tolerance were the inherent pitfalls of any program aiming to limit intake of substances "by supplying small amounts to take the edge off the urge for more." And so Holland's program failed. The meager clinical and statistical evidence from their programs reveals how loosely they were regulated (38,83,84). In addition to Holland, other countries such as Belgium, Switzerland, and Australia recently considered returning to heroin maintenance despite cautions from history and empirical evidence.

Detoxification, the only specific treatment procedure in addiction, is called "going for the cure" by addicts. To them this means reducing their level of physical dependence, or "getting clean for the moment." In reality, withdrawal only produces an unstable drug-free state which is neither "well" nor cured. "Cure," Medical Officer in Charge of Narco, J.D. Reichard emphasized (90), "should never, or only rarely, be used in assessing addiction treatment results. In the medical context 'cure' means that the cause of an illness has been removed; detoxification, the elimination of physical dependence, temporarily removes a consequence of use, not the cause. One should not call a detoxified abuser of any substance a cured person; instead he should be referred to as "discharged as drug free." Nor, should he be turned loose on the public as an expert advocate of some treatment mode, any more than a recovered cardiac patient would be considered an expert in heart disease equipped to advise heart patients of a proper course of treatment.

Methadone-maintenance programs were born in the United States during the Nixon administration under a cloud of political expediency. Government advisers, experts perhaps in political policy making, were not experts in policies to prevent or treat drug abuse. Their programs against drug abuse had been based on the theory that "drugs take people," not "people take drugs" (50). The Nixon Administration confusing the efficacy of "methadone detoxification" with "methadone maintenance" supported an ill-advised recommendation for "methadone maintenance therapy as a cure for heroin addiction" (19,20). The methadone program was introduced against Narco's advice during the Nixon administration's need for a political mission that would be popular with voting public. With a change in the rules of the game and obfuscating media talk that methadone "blockades against heroin," an illusory cure for opiate addiction was sold to the public. Narco countered against the advocates' false claims. "Don't take this substitute, it's the real thing"! but failed to convince the public and especially youth to reject methadone maintenance. Instead of preventing relapse by "blockade," as claimed by its advocates, methadone prevented abstinence by perpetuating narcotic use.

The chaos of methadone maintenance, now big business with a vast community of dependent users in a widespread government-endorsed program, was accurately predicted. In 1996, the National Science Council suggested scrapping the programs! If that came to pass, physically dependent methadone users "begging for a fix" would crowd the streets! Hidden behind media and public relations smoke-screens was the untold story of methadone and physical dependence. The drug's diversion into a black market had led to closure of many clinics and the curtailing of programs in the United States. Though called the "most despised treatment in the United States" by Dr. Herbert Kleber of Columbia University, methadone maintenance remains the most prescribed procedure.

Comparing opiate and methadone maintenance

The typical compulsive morphinist injects, "mainlines," his drug into a vein. Within a few seconds his pupils constrict; an initial orgasmic "rush" is felt; a sense of well-being called "straight" or "feeling normal" embraces him. The addict now "fixed" goes on the "nod," drifting in and out of sleep, experiencing wish-fulfilling reveries. Abrupt stoppage of the narcotic in a physicaly dependent person leads to the gooseflesh, profuse perspiration, and complaints of chills and muscle pains, of the "cold turkey."

Methadone's daily maintenance dose of 80 to 120 mgms. is four to six times larger than the therapeutic dose. Claimed to produce a uniform plateau of "straight time without reverie," a 20 mgm. oral dose would sedate a compulsive abuser into deep-dreaming sleep. If 80 mgm. had been the first exposure it would likely have been the last. Without the gradual build-up of tolerance and accompanying physical dependence, collapse of the respiratory and circulatory systems would cause death. Since intravenous methadone also produces the "rush" and "nod," it loses its principal value for maintenance and a normal lifestyle. Long-acting methadone was developed hopefully to eliminate these effects but could not influence the reactions.

Claims of methadone maintenance's efficacy

Methadone maintenance is alleged to prevent relapse to heroin, reduce criminal activity, improve vocational and social adjustment, and reduce the use of illicit drugs. How does methadone do this? Does methadone reduce criminal behavior through its pharmacological properties, or is the reduction in criminal behavior a result of changing the rules of the game? Buying an illegal substance means trafficking with criminals and criminal activity. Supply the same substance legally, at little or no cost, then the need for petty thievery to "scramble for a fix" is hopefully eliminated. Therefore, addicts maintained legally on opiates or methadone have a lower number of arrests. Furthermore, certain types of aggressive delinquents stop their criminal activity while using narcotics. New York city's fighting gangs in the 50s melted away as the individual members turned to the increasingly available heroin. As one former Gang Lord put it,"I haven't been in a rumble since I found horse" (heroin).

The high daily doses required in either maintenance program produce the "fix" or "nod." The patients' complaints that methadone (as with opiates) "gets into your marrow and takes away your manhood" is well founded. Receiving narcotics sufficient to satisfy craving for the intoxication, the abuser is "fixed," (an appropriate term that is also used as a euphemism for castration), showing no interest in sex, aggression, or food. In clinics of municipal hospitals and to private physicians, mates complained that their husbands or wives on methadone avoided not only their sexual relationship but responsible participation as parents generally. Thus, a patient who reports faithfully to the methadone clinic and returns home to watch television, oblivious to family, is recorded as one who has ceased theft, robbery, and trafficking in illegal drugs. If he or she works or attends school, another statistical column swells with pride.

Shifting focus from study of statistics of improved job and school attendance to clinical observation reveals a different picture. Mathematical statements of social functioning do not register crucial interpersonal relationships. What sort of children do such passive, drugged, rejecting, non-participating parents raise? Among other things, children and adolescents with greater interest in the lure of drugs. Government approval of maintenance also seductively encourages adolescents confronted by their painful developmental conflicts of urges and controls to find relief in drugs.

Premature uncritical acceptance of maintenance programs has had its predictable consequences. Black market traffic, abusive use, fatal overdoses are with us. The fact is methadone does not prevent relapse. It prevents abstinence by maintaining a narcotic fix! Inflated promises have paid off in disillusionment (67,68). In 1972 when both private and public maintenance treatment centers were flourishing, an article in the New York Times began, "Drug abuse treatment has blossomed into a billion dollar national industry with an ambiguous clientele and an uncertain product"(67). This was a new tune for some of the original supporters of the program.

Compulsive abusers rarely seek therapy, other than to momentarily reduce their physical dependence (10). In treatment, generally, the release of inhibitions is more acceptable to patients than self-imposed restrictions on compulsive behavior. The struggle of a normal person to diet and lose a few pounds, or stop smoking, though stressful, is a shadow compared to a compulsive eater's or smoker's distress while reducing the intake of food or tobacco. As any Type 2 or 3 begins to restrict a compulsive symptom, the need for relief becomes urgent and relapse occurs. And must be expected to recur until psychological changes that represent healing permit self-control over the symptom. The community and government agencies are not prepared to "support relapse as part of the struggle for health." They want to believe that "well" means "being dry or clean" at the start, instead of at the end of the psychological struggle to eliminate the need for the symptom.

Drug free, the user is most vulnerable for relapse until emotionally well, so relapse must not be judged as it usually is, as a willful refusal of help. The freedom to relapse to a drug of choice may save an abuser's life. Has it been decided that "drug use," which now may include alcohol and tobacco is a criminal activity, a social illness symptom, a reaction to economic stress, a sign of psychiatric illness, or even a normal activity? All categories are, in fact, possible considerations.

Curtailment and enforcement theory flaws

Laws serve community demands not the mental health needs of the individual. When law enforcement methods entered the field of treatment of drug abuse they paralleled punishment. Frustrated with continued lack of success the crusaders' approach to "cure and control" of substance abuse became a frenzy of escalating punishment. The government's punitive efforts to stop smuggling masqueraded as therapy. In addition early proposals to report users to a central medical registry, as practiced with measles or venereal disease, were enacted against the advice of the USPHS and New York City Health department in the 1950s. Their predictions that patients would disappear from health care centers and equate their doctors with police were confirmed.

It was proposed to set up a boycott of the drug supply and increase punishment for infractions to discourage users. This strategy, naively applied to the drug world, ignored the history of the birth of drugs.

In this War the war chest of the enemy is limitless, while the crusader's is finite. The loss of a ton of cannabis or one million dollars of cocaine means little to the syndicates, but the cost of capturing a few kilos of drugs or a supplier or two is astronomical. The "President's

Commission Report On Crime" refuted the popular opinion that a close, causal relationship existed between opiate addicts and the high cost of crime to society. The over-riding cost relationship to crime, it was found, did not come from the petty crimes committed by abusers, but from costs of enforcement of laws to control smuggling and trafficking by international organized crime syndicates.

Is the eradication of a substance a proven method of stopping abuse? All of the evidence says "No." When the supply of any substance had been interrupted or was in short supply, crime syndicates were quick to switch and supply whatever replacements that the public had substituted. As examples, cocaine is not the only substance that acts like cocaine and can be substituted with methedrine; methadone was created during World War 2 after Germany was cut off from its Turkish supplier of medically destined morphine; bathroom gin appeared and kept "booze" available during Prohibition days in the United States. The Volstead Act spurred bootlegging and racketeering while "Corn likker" home brews flourished in the "mountain stills." An unlimited supply of substitutes replaced scarce items; as examples, methedrine replaced benzidrine; tranquilizers replaced barbiturates, as occurred with a wide variety of substances (74).

After detoxification, drug-using patients have the same diagnostic classifications as non-drug-using patients. No mass therapeutic approach can apply to all. No more can be done for the drug-using group of patients than for the non-users. The hard fact is that no new or successful treatment modalities for substance abusers, other than detoxification techniques, have been forthcoming since Narco's time. Treatment for abusers remains as for psychiatric patients in general and, unfortunately, the reliance on psychotropic medications as "therapy" will continue the dependence on substances.

Shadows on the world horizon should cause public concern. Insurance companies still determine a patient's therapeutic needs by payment clauses that limit psychotherapy. Compliant psychiatrists are now "pushing drugs" and thereby encouraging dependence on them. Ominously, in the training of psychiatrists a marked retreat from teaching and encouraging psychotherapy has led to a corresponding increase in emphasis and reliance on psychotropic medications. This bodes ill for the future of psychological treatment. Thankfully, however, a revolt by patients and their doctors to eliminate the insurance companies' dictates and payment restrictions has occurred. "We would prefer to pay our bills ourselves and be able to talk to our doctors instead of taking pills" is the new patient stance.

The first page topics of the May 15th, 1998 issue of Psychiatric News are: "NIDA to focus research on drug abuse in children"; and "APA, AACAP praise testing of psychotropics for children." That research is in the hands of neuro-scientists looking for genetic factors to treat with drugs. The "praise" is pointedly reversed years later. A feature article in the January 19th 2000 edition Of Psychiatric News states "Joining the American Psychiatric Association, the American Academy of Child and Adolescent Psychiatry, and the American Academy of Pediatrics, the American Medical Association adopted a new policy calling on the pharmaceutical industry and federal regulators to study the effects of psychotropic drugs on children and acknowledged the need for training of additional qualified clinical investigators to do so. With few exceptions the evidence for safety and efficacy of psychotropic medications when used with children (and adults too) is based solely on anecdotal accounts" (in other words, not through scientific method). Many psychiatrists and psychoanalysts who had not been in tune with the controversial concepts were demeaned and called "drugless doctors." Drug therapy advocates, by abandoning basic psychological findings of the past, seem to view patients as dehumanized neuro-chemical structures.

While the "War Against Drugs" stagnated, a private venture group (25) searched for a pill (potion) that when taken daily would block the need to take pills (potions) daily. A distorted logic then claimed this would immunize children against the need to take drugs daily!!

Antabuse pills were to prevent an alcoholic from drinking; Naltrexone was to deter a morphinist from opium; methadone, a narcotic, was to suppress the need to take narcotics by daily use of a narcotic. A pill is currently being marketed to overcome shyness in children. Anti-obesity pills, diet control potions, along with laxatives, and anti-nicotine potions abound in the community.

2

Adolescence

History of adolescence

Adolescence is a psychological phase of life; adolescents are the youths, the primary targets of "drug program" planners. Adolescence, seemingly an a straight forward term, usually refers to a period of life, roughly ranging from 13 to 21 years of age, between childhood and adulthood. This is an everyday common, identification but is far too loose for scientific discussion.But as a developmental phase of life, adolescence holds an ambiguous place. In 1962 Aries (2) described how the child in the Middle Ages was regarded simply as a small adult who only slowly emerged as a distinct social entity. Until the 19th century children would pass from childhood to adulthood with no special recognition of an adolescent status. As civilization progressed, a time gap between childhood and adulthood was introduced and widened by each culture's or community's needs for the skills of both youth and adult. It seems that as societies became more complex an interlude of apprenticeship developed restricting expression of biological maturity until a legal age of adulthood set by the elders was reached. A prolonged adolescence created by society's controls is a relatively recent phenomenon.

Adolescence, as modern society knows it, has not always been with us, and its form and duration varies throughout the world. According to Stone and Church (103) there is no equivalent in primitive society for the modern industrial world's concept of adolescence. In many primitive cultures the transition from childhood to adulthood is so smooth that it goes unrecognized. "More frequently we find that the young person on the threshold of physical maturity goes through a ceremonial adolescence called a puberty rite, timed with the onset of sexual maturity (103)." Puberty rites signaled the end of childhood and entrance into young adulthood with all privileges and responsibilities of adulthood such as the traditions of each society dictated.

The 1900s were called the "century of the adolescent" (2). "The most casual observervation of the contemporary cultural scene in the industrialized world will reveal the dominant influence of adolescents and youth on styles of dress, popular entertainment and recreation, food consumption and, often, political life. Selma, Columbia, Kent State, or Nanterre demonstrate youth's potential for dramatic and, at times violent efforts at social change. Literary depictions of adolescence have abounded since the Romantic Age; Young Werther set the tone of reminiscences of youthful self discovery. Shakespeare had long ago provided classical representations of various aspects of the adolescent experience. 'Romeo and Juliet' embodies as no other work the romantic ardor of adolescent passion. The saga of young Henry, Prince of Wales' emergence into King Henry V is a virtual textbook demonstration of identity formation in an older adolescent responding to developmental crisis. In our time James Joyce, Thomas Mann, J.D. Salinger, Carson McCullers, and Erik Erikson exemplify this continuing literary tradition" (22).

The scientific study of the psychology of adolescence is distinctly a product of the Twentieth Century, and can be said to coincide with the growth of psychoanalysis both as a method of investigation and as a theoretical system. Although Gesell, Ames, Piaget, Margaret Meade, Schoenfeld in other disciplines have made monumental contributions towards clarification of human developmental norms, it is fair to say that only psychoanalysts have introduced the knowledge of the personal inner psychological experience of adolescence and the psychic transformations it entails.

A definition of "adolescence" was difficult to establish. Edith Jacobson (47) poetically described adolescence as "a life between a saddening farewell to childhood, and a gradual, anxious, hopeful passing over many barriers to the gates that permit entry into the unknown country of adulthood." Piaget (80) described adolescence, "As the age when the individual becomes integrated into the society of adults, the age when the child no longer feels he is below the level of his elders, but equal, at least in rights to the adult." This integration into adult society has many emotional links to puberty. It also includes very profound intellectual changes. Piaget stressed that the intellectual changes represent the achievement of an entire process of evolution that originates at birth and whose stages can be observed throughout the development of the child. Freud described adolescence as if it were synonymous with puberty as the time when changes set in that gave sexual life its final form.

Psychological studies of adolescents began in 1905 with Sigmund Freud's "Three essays on the Theory of Sexuality" (33). His series of essays were followed by many other pioneering psychoanalytic investigators, such as Aichorn (1), Bernfeld (7), Hartmann (39), A. Freud (30), Bornstein (11), Erikson (25). Mahler's studies of infants and children detailed the linked transitional phases of the psychological path of development from babyhood to adolescence (65,66).

Adolescence and puberty

Although now generally accepted as a psychological state of change, adolescence was originally considered synonymous with "puberty," a physical state of change. Dated by the physical signs of a boy's first ejac-ulation and a girl's menstruation, puberty traditionally signified the attainment of biological maturity. Observable changes in growth, body configuration, physiology, and endocrine effects are actually visible and measurable long before ejaculation or menstruation appear (117). Refinement of observation revealed that first menstruations are gener-ally anovulatory and ejaculations aspermic. Therefore, if reproductive maturity was the essential characteristic of puberty, these "firsts" were not conclusive evidence of it. Some controversy developed over what observable changes should be considered the initial herald of puberty. Ultimately the decision depended on the observers' preferred criteria. However, consensus and tradition still retain menarche and ejaculation as the hallmarks of the onset of puberty timing the pubertal rites of passage.

Both Bernfeld (8) and Anna Freud (30) have maintained that adoles-cence is less well understood from the viewpoint of psychological and sexual development than childhood. "One of the reasons for the insuffi-ciency of scientific literature of this period is to be found in the great multiplicity of phenomena of this age" (8). Their fear of the breakdown of the psychological barriers that had been erected against sexual and hostile aggression during latency accounts for adolescents' innumerable behavioral phenomena. This fact has made a uniform description of adolescence difficult.

Bernfeld attempted to delineate two groups of youths by their reac-tions to their drive changes of puberty. One, he called the neurotic group, was characterized by anxiety and defenses that try to deny their pubertal changes and to live as if nothing happened. Anxiety is the cen-tral psychological feature of this group. The cause of the anxiety is to be found in the early years of childhood when barriers against sexuality are first erected. The signs of beginning sexual maturity threatens these barriers. The second group takes a positive and affirmative attitude to the first signs of sexual maturity. These young people behave as if they had desired and yearned for sexual maturity for a long time, and comprise a group he called uncomplicated, simple puberty. The contrast between the two groups, Bernfeld maintained, was based on the condition that the ideal of being grown up remained unbroken throughout childhood. Latency had been a period of impatient waiting for them. The first signs of awakening sexual maturity are greeted with a wave of increased self esteem, "now I am grown up." Society, however, by opposing adolescent sexual activities aggravates youths' defiant rebelliousness to disobey restrictions, coarsening their sexual lives.

Since adolescence is a fluid process, not a static condition, an adolescent may change behavior from one type to another in the course of a few years. Different cultures permit, prohibit, or frustrate gratification of the maturing biological drives. The ensuing conflicts, that develop both intra-psychically and inter-personally, will prolong childhood or delay onset of adolescence. In that context, adolescence has been considered a "cultural invention" (103). The abstinence which society attempts to impose produces irritability and anxiety which, as additions to the aggression normally biologically present, sets the stage for smoldering anti-social, rebellious behavior to flame up. Of the varieties of adolescent disturbance, the most characteristic and certainly the most socially significant is delinquency, or antisocial behavior.

The pioneer in the psychoanalytic study of delinquency was the Viennese educator and lawyer, August Aichorn (1). He wrote (21, p.230), "Although we must guard against generalization, our studies seem to justify the formulation of general principles of causation. Delinquency represents one of the departures from the normal psychic development, and for this reason a solution of the problem of delinquents depends on understanding their mental contents. We know that antisocial behavior is the result of disturbed psychic patterns, of abnormal accumulations of affect (emotion). The manner in which the psychic energy is utilized determines the direction in which the individual develops; whether he will be psychologically normal, whether he will be subject to nervous illness, or whether he will become asocial. Since our generalized explanations and conclusions about the delinquents' psychology may, up to now, seem obvious, you may underestimate the necessity for a thorough psychological study of each youth. You may even believe that you can simply adopt a few psychological principles and carry on your work (treatment of disturbed adolescents) as formerly, before psychoanalytic study. Such an idea would lead you to dilettantism which is worse than ignorance. You must be guided by sound theoretical knowledge or your efforts are doomed to fail."

Adolescence is a period of a youth's prolonged and often painful self-involvement. A number of contradictory attitudes and behavioral patterns develop, such as gregariousness and solitariness, indulgence and asceticism, altruism and bigotry. These arise from the characteristic adolescent conflicts over their drives and the need to control them. Such widely self-contradictory attitudes would suggest that a psychiatric disorder, such as an initial phase of a psychosis, would need to be present that could make these mental contradictions tolerable even to the youth.

The consensus of specialists' opinions is that psychological treatment of adolescents at different stages of development is most difficult, and requires special modifications of procedure at those times. The appropriate phase behavior of rebellion against adults creates in the youth the belief that treatment of any sort is an entrapment. This attitude aggravates both the adolescents' fight for emancipation, and their unstable hold on reality. These factors add to their illogic that resists allowing the needed relationship. Their resistance may be softened and then return at different moments. Therefore therapeutic interventions are often stop and go, a biding of time as phases modify. Treatment and development of programs for adolescent drug users must take into consideration many diverse vacillating forms of resistance. At one moment mature at another childish they react to their specific phase-induced stresses with varieties of rapidly changing regressive behaviors that

bewilder adults. Talented and trained personnel are of primary importance in treating disturbed youths in this group.

Prepuberty and preadolescence

The constellation of physical and physiological maturational changes
which precede menarche and ejaculation has been designated "prepuberty" for descriptive, chronological purposes. Prepuberty begins and is
recognizable in children between the ages of ten and twelve years. Girls'
breasts develop, boys' penises and testicles enlarge, nipples in both sexes
may become sensitive, and pubic hair appears. On the average girls tend
to show changes earlier than boys, menarche appearing shortly after the
13th birthday, while ejaculation occurs shortly before the 14th.

Preadolescence has psychological characteristics which set it apart
from the latency period at the end of childhood, and the beginning of
adolescence. The prepubertal increase in hormonal levels influences
"preadolescence," the accompanying psychological state. Prepuberty
and preadolescence are inter-related just as puberty and adolescence
are. The drive thrusts of the prepubertal and pubertal phases of maturation upset the relative calm of late latency. Preadolescence is set apart
from latency and adolescence by its special psychological and behavioral   characteristics   (5,6,17,21,47,51,60,100).   The   psychological
defenses that had been erected against the sexual drives and aims characteristic for childhood weaken. Psychological unrest then follows.

The onset of fidgetiness, touching compulsions, sleep disturbances,
overconcern with body functions, and the altered relationship between
boys and girls physically signify the end of latency. A number of other
symptoms occur in both sexes. Fainting, feelings of unreality, excessive
sleepiness, gluttony and anorexia, and disturbances of motility frequently appear.

A particularly interesting characteristic of preadolescence is the change in relationship between boys and girls. Open warfare between them replaces the peaceful coexistence and relative freedom to tolerate sexual feelings and fantasies that existed during the latency period. Preadolescents find themselves in the throes of hateful feelings of aversion and sadistic tendencies toward children of the opposite sex. Nuances of enjoyable relationships between the sexes will mark the entrance into early adolescence and beyond. A behavioral passivity in boys may alternate with greater motoric activity as responses to the intensifying sexual and aggressive urges. In addition, boys become interested in testicular size and motility and penile changes, but their major concerns focus on their sense of passivity vis-a-vis females who are viewed as taller and overpowering, and in the jargon "phallic." Girls, fearing their own sexual yearnings, become activity oriented "like tomboys." School work often undergoes a transient but turbulent phase of decline in both sexes, underscoring the seventh graders' reputation for creating problems with teachers and being the hardest to teach. Illogic, daydreaming, and difficulty in concentrating on learning tasks interfere with academic achievement. Paradoxically, the preadolescents also increase their capacity for greater abstraction at the same time.

An overt clash between child and parents marks the beginning of emotional detachment on the road to adolescence and adulthood. The child's defiance serves two ends: it creates an illusion of emancipation and self-sufficiency from the adults, and it defends against their intensified sensual life. At this age sexual urges directed at the parents are, more than ever, taboo. Sexuality will have acquired a more genital, adult quality to their fantasies that then create marked guilt and anxiety. The child's need to detach from parents then becomes more urgent and regressions often intervene as palliatives. Studies of the differences between adolescence and childhood have enriched knowledge of the psychological maturation timetable, just as earlier studies had illuminated the path of sexual development.

But to conceive of the psychological changes as simple reactions to hormonal changes is misleading. Adolescence possesses psychological characteristics and developmental tasks which distinguish it from pre-adolescence on the one hand,and adulthood on the other (10,30,44,51). Adolescence is now defined in terms of psychological maturational tasks and stages, as a series of phases. Blos (10) has established that, "each adolescent phase can be described and delineated along three lines, namely in terms of typical drives and controls; an integral conflict between them; and a developmental task to be completed." Such, for example, as emancipating from the "incestuous objects" or family members. This task has at least three stages. After sexual drive takes on more adult qualities, the masturbatory fantasies with their incestuous images arouse more guilt and anxiety. The images are then exchanged for others, but although realistically outside of the family circle they reveal poorly concealed "incestuous" connections. With further development, attachment to other non-incestuous people with more disguise initiates the final emancipation from home. A strict biological timetable or age, such as between fourteen years and the early twenties, for the beginning and ending of adolescence or preadolescence is thereby avoided.

Youth and drugs

What can be said about adolescent drug use? Not very much if observational focus is limited to just the symptom of use. A basically healthy teenager may show alarming symptoms which often disappear spontaneously. A youth with an intact personality may use drugs, while a disturbed youngster may not. The significant differences between those who do and those who do not use drugs is unclear. Because of confusion in terminology and the unreliability of many statistic gathering methods, the extent of normal teenager drug use is unknown. We don't know exactly how many normal teenagers use or abuse drugs. Irrational public hysteria has placed all drugs, all adolescents, and all use into one bag. What can be said, however, is that young people who sustain a relationship with severely regressive intoxicants and persist in seeking regression, had serious childhood psychological problems before adolescence or drug use began. Those psychological disturbances are not the average "normals" of children or adolescents. They are not average teenagers and will not develop into average adults.

"Normal and abnormal"

Pathology and normalcy are assessment or evaluative terms. Freud (36) noted, "No sharp line can be drawn between neurotic and normal people. Our conception of disease is a purely practical one and a question of summation: predisposition and the eventualities of life must combine before the threshold is overstepped. Pathology, a modification of health, is rooted in developmental patterning and may be considered as an exaggeration or inhibition of some normal mental function. Pathological symptoms do not erupt from barren ground, but emerge from a developmental root and model."

Anna Freud (31) elaborated, "The demarcation between mental health and illness is even more difficult to draw in childhood and adolescence than in later stages. In a child's growth toward maturity it is inherent that the proportion of strength between drives and mental development is in constant flux; that the adaptive and defensive, beneficial and pathogenic processes merge with each other; that the transitions from one developmental level to the next constitute points of potential arrest, malfunction, fixation, and regression; drives and mentality develop at different rates; in short, a number of factors combine

to undermine, arrest, and distort the forces on which healthy development is based."

The emotional coming to terms with their maturing genitals and sec-
ondary sexual characteristics that lead to a change in their body image
is a gradual and conflict-ridden process. The pubic and armpit hair and
breasts become a source of conflict in both sexes. To become a man or a
woman may then represent a displacement from genitals to having the
hair. The acceptance of a sexually competent penis may be gradual in
the boy. The loss of control in involuntary erections and nocturnal
emissions, "wet dreams," is a severe humiliation to the male adolescent,
reminiscent of earlier enuresis embarrassments.

Masturbation may either begin or stop with the first menarche. The
task to be achieved by the adolescent girl to attain her femininity
requires she shift interest from the clitoris to the vagina, and secondly
from activity to passivity to "receive" the penis. The first menstruation,
often experienced as an injury and punishment depending on earlier
education in sexual matters by the parents, may either support the
trend to "feminine" or rejection of femininity. Characteristic of the
young girl's erotic longing is the expectation of a sexual experience as
distinct from motherhood, called the double sexual role of woman-
hood, namely that of mother and lover. Only later and gradually, perhaps not until sexual intercourse has taken place, do the two tendencies
become closely interwoven, either mutually supportive or in conflict
with one another.

It is generally accepted today that moderate indulgence in masturbation with full awareness of the action, its associated fantasies, and with
attainment of orgasm is not harmful, as myths would have it.
Compulsive, excessive masturbation, however, does indicate that psychopathology is present. Through a violent internal struggle the youth
may stop masturbating entirely in an attempt to control the accompanying incestuous fantasies and become ascetic. Or, will completely suppress

the fantasies and impair personality development by eliminating a fantasy life of creativity.

The scientific literature lacks any explicit discussion of whether sexual intercourse in adolescence is healthy or unhealthy and of whether it could alleviate the enormous tension of that period. Bernfeld pointed out that adolescents seeking sexual intercourse must face the strong opposition of society and consequently their sexuality becomes significantly coarsened. Helene Deutsch claims the same in respect to girls. An incapacity to tolerate their own ambivalence to the opposite sex, the polarities of love and hate, leads to a "breakdown" of thinking repeatedly and the whole period of adolescence becomes a series of neurotic and at times psychotic states. Decisive and permanent changes occur during those moments. However the adolescent turmoil and its accompanying psychological reorganization have been viewed as "a second chance" to mature, heal, and rectify earlier faults of development. This is true for many adolescents, even for those with florid symptoms.

Factors favoring use of drugs

Adolescence lays bare the flaws of faulty development and is the time when these consequences cannot be evaded (50). Their painful mental states arise in the emotional conflicts engendered by urgent simultaneous claims of biological drives, reality, and conscience. The pain and turmoil are mitigated when regression turns off either the impulses or their inhibitors so that reality or conscience may temporarily be ignored. Maturity, however, is forged in conflict, and continuing regression from the inner conflicts perpetuates immaturity, psychological dependency, and passivity. Young people who persist in deep, drug-induced regressions reveal flawed development that was present before adolescence or exposure to drugs.

A difficulty to tolerate waiting, to control impulses, to endure frustration typify the disturbed personalities. The acquisition of these qualities necessary to bear and deal psychologically with conflict begins in early childhood years of development. Adolescents who fail to develop them adequately may then crave that which will release them from the suffering of their disturbed states. Until adult maturity is attained, adolescents' drug use always is of Type 2 or 3. The earlier in age that the compulsion appears, the more probable it is that underlying severe psychopathology is present. The younger adolescent feels more weakened and unequal vis-a-vis his or her awakened drives and impulses. The inner forces opposing regression are undeveloped favoring the appeal of magic relief by a drug that is imagined as the powerful ally to help them in their struggles.

Adolescent coping behavior

Apart from substance abuse, young teenagers have numerous and characteristic ways to cope with their stresses. They band together as an emotional support to ease the loneliness and depression associated with their psychological disengagement from the parents. To re-enforce their group membership they adopt a badge of conformity, which for some, but not all, may be drug use. Superficial, conscious reasons such as curiosity, experimentation, and peer group pressures are often presented as the motives for use. Smoking and drinking often consciously represent adult behavior in the teenager's mind. Many young people, by pretending to use and by exaggerating their involvement with substances, symbolically try to create an adult image, or find group acceptance, or even gain entry into a drug program to establish a feeling of belonging. It is an encouraging prognostic sign if the symbolism in the drug connection is more important than the regressive experience from its use.

The motivations supplied by unconscious symbolic meanings of use or substance are not frequently mentioned. A substance may symbolically represent a person, or part of a person that the user wants to possess or be possessed by; to control or to be controlled by. Drug use may symbolize an attack on someone else. A substance may symbolize defiance and exclusion of the adult from the now secret rites of the adolescent. Other less conscious motives may center around thoughts of defying death, courting death, and acting out suicidal fantasies. Recoiling in terror from approaching maturity and confronted with mortality, defensively they may strike a pose of invulnerability to death. The way they drive, recklessly swallow, inhale, or ingest all manner of substances, or are driven to life-endangering games and hobbies is death defying. The symbolic act may mean, "If I show I am not afraid of death, then I won't die." Trying to invite death to erase the suspense of when death will occur is also encountered. Suicidal motives may derive from deep feelings of hatred for the self or others, or from guilt. As the ultimate revenge against a hated parent, suicide may also represent fulfillment of a wish to join a lost, loved one. A secret experience with a substance far below lethal dosage, as with aspirin, can signify a symbolic brush with death.

The literature on suicide in children and adolescence is sparse, but Gould (in 22) has surveyed the studies and reports a consensus that suicide is a multidetermined symptom representing an unsuccessful effort to resolve conflicts and tension states. The many reasons for suicidal behavior are directly related to physical, intellectual, and psychological levels of development. Children have a very incomplete, distorted concept of death, for example, which they often see as a reversible process. Distortion also occurs through cultural attitudes of the parents who "soften" the blow of death's finality by equating it to "sleep." Gould postulates various "types of suicides": as a wish to gain support and strength through joining the powerful but lost loved one; or as a retaliation for a rejection or threat of abandonment; as atonement for guilt; and more. From the myriad of precipitating causes, the underlying fears of rejection or deprivation dominate as important factors.

The young try on many roles, identify with numerous heroes who may even be criminals, accept and reject different causes or ideals, and shuffle relationships. They experiment, sample, taste, and discard more choices and ambitions than they can keep. If adolescents appear to be promiscuous with all drugs this is a misperception. They put drugs, relationships, ambitions through the same process of searching, sampling, and discarding. Their range of preferences and options in life narrows as definitive choices must be made on the march to adulthood. Ultimate choices must be consciously satisfying and fulfill deeper unconscious needs. Maturity eliminates many options so that fewer intoxications retain appeal, but attraction to alcohol or cannabis in a Type 1 manner as adults may remain.

A crucial influence that is missing from these young peoples' lives is steadfast parenting. There are parents with severe psychological disturbances; others who over-medicate themselves and their children; some cannot let their children endure frustration or discipline; others are in unrewarding marriages; or have been deserted; others are overwhelmed by the adolescent's turmoil; many of the parents are little more than unenlightened adolescents themselves.

The youth with adequate development throughout childhood does not crave regression. Prolonged regression is experienced as an intolerable enslavement. Nevertheless, regressions do occur, with or without drugs. But the normal adolescent opposes his regressions with the progressive forces in his or her personality, even if not as forcefully as an adult. These include wishes to grow up into autonomous adulthood, to find meaningful and intimate relationships. Such an adolescent keeps returning from limited regression and drugs fade from center stage.

1952 conferences on adolescents

In 1952 conferences on "Drug addiction among adolescents" were hosted by The New York Academy of Medicine and cosponsored by The Welfare Council of New York, an organization of representatives from law, medicine, education, and social sciences. The discussions highlighted the absence of consensus. The Welfare Council (107) presented their report, "a description of the progress made by the Council's committee on Use of Narcotics Among Teen-Age Youth. It tells of a plan of action which, when carried to completion will destroy this menace." Certainly a noble intent but a repetitive, unrealistic one!

Programs to "wipe out drugs that are destroying our youth" were presented by talented people from the various disciplines in familiar terminology (107), but each with their own frame of reference. Law and order sector viewed drug problem as the illegal trade or possession of proscribed substances. Social scientists blamed enviornmental stress as the cause of abuse. The medical representatives continued the somatic toxin theory. Everyone's aim was to "stamp out drugs," but in the absence of unifying conceptualization, no collaborative effort was possible since each discipline vied for dominance. The Welfare Council complained that the many differences of opinions and contradictory conclusions sabotaged any attempts to create a workable hypothesis.

Dr. Haven Emerson (23), a former Commissioner of Health of New York City discussed a "new" clinical observation of 1952."If I am not mistaken," he said, "we are now experiencing another large epidemic of drug addiction. I think we had one in 1911 and again in 1922. We first became aware of a new group of young people addicted to heroin flowing through the alcoholic ward at Bellevue Hospital. I assure you the same thoughts, the same plans, the same social concerns confronting us today in 1952 existed forty years ago." Adolescents from age fifteen to twenty-one were stated to be vulnerable to this problem as if by contagion, hence the term "epidemic," and also were alleged to be a new wave of addicts. Yet in 1940 Narco's statistics revealed that thirty per cent of their admissions started their relationship to drugs while still under the age of eighteen.

Why are there such passionate, futile attempts to save the world and change human nature? Apart from the saccharinized, banal response, "To save our youth or country," which drug-use control will never do, no answers other than those couched in sanctimonious and economic terms have been heard. Knowing Man's psychology, is it possible to have a drug free world? Is it even necessary? Assuming this theoretical "drug-free"world, mental health would be no better since aberrations would find other forms of expression. Surely more suicide, psychosis, and violence among Types 2 and 3 personalities would develop. And someone would create potions anyway.

Faults in programs to suppress drug use in adolescents

All of the existing or proposed therapeutic programs for drug abuse and adolescent involvement contain primary significant faults. Any therapeutic venture dignified as "rational" must begin with a thorough diagnostic evaluation, before goals and procedures are individualized to the unique combination of each adult or adolescent person's assets and liabilities. This has been neglected in past and ongoing programs. Research, diagnosis, treatment all require talented, trained, and experienced personnel, in addition to adequately funded and staffed facilities and a personnel-training infrastructure. The absence of these necessaries along with simplistic theories make current projects worthless. Since similar-appearing compulsive behavior can represent different motivations or causes, mass-scale approaches are predictably doomed to fail.

3

Illiteracy

Background information

The preschool child's capacity for learning and social development was increasingly recognized by those who saw learning as a continuum. They stressed that free thinking and curiosity, even about sexual matters, is essential for productive learning. "Among creative educators, John Dewey (1902) and Maria Montessori (1909) were preeminent. While differing in some respects about educational principles both stressed that the child is only motivated to learn when the material is meaningfully related to his own experience—in the case of the young child, his experience as a member of the family. While Freud clarified the ways in which internal processes can inhibit learning, Dewey and Montessori drew attention to external interferences which stemmed from some traditional teaching methods, such as enforced passivity in the classroom, inappropriate material, and mass instruction. Before and during World War 1, Montessori's methods stirred much interest in Europe and the United States. In 1917 the analytic group in Vienna shared Freud's interest and planned to establish a Montessori institute. A bond existed between analytic thinking and education" (22).

Freud's early papers (34,36) had important implications for parents and educators. He discussed the ways that children seek from infancy, according to their developmental age, drive satisfaction from the parents. He illustrated the ways in which the manner that drive expressions, particularly sexual and aggressive, had been handled in young children affected the child's ability to learn. "Education had previously set itself the task of controlling, or suppressing the drives. Nor has anyone enquired by what means and at what cost the suppression of the inconvenient drives has been achieved. The results have by no means been gratifying. Supposing now that we, as parents and teachers, substitute a different task. Instead of suppressing drives, we should aim instead at making the individual capable of becoming a civilized and useful member of society with the least possible sacrifice of his own activity" (33). The relationship of the sexual drive was recognized by Freud as most significant for learning. He noted that historians of civilization had customarily regarded cultural achievements as "a diversion of sexual instincts from overt sexual aims and changed their direction to new aims—a process which deserves the name of sublimation" (1909). Freud's unique contribution was to relate the same process to the development of the individual. He also recognized the appearance of sublimation as the beginning of latency and traced and compared outcomes from energetic suppressive means of the drives, namely "neurotic inhibition and sexualization of thinking." According to the outcome from an exaggerated suppression, Freud suggested a person's ability to think freely could be affected for a lifetime.

Learning, a widely used term, cannot be adequately defined. However we can conceive of a learning function emerging from an assumed innate capacity to learn. The learning function, a superordinate structure, is itself the result of a highly complex mix of mental functions, that organizes other mental components such as drive energy, perception, retention, recall into systems that serve the ends of Man's mastery of life and survival. As is the case with the more inclusive function of intellectuality to which it contributes, the development of the learning function can be traced from its early emergence in the mother-child relationship to its highly specialized activity of independent academic pursuits. Anna Freud (31) emphasized that the "first and most important step in the direction of mastery (of self and environment) is the association of drives with words, a process called the 'intellectualization of the instinctual life'. The connecting of impulses with ideas that can be dealt with in the mind with words in place of action, is one of the most general, earliest, and most necessary acquirements of the human mind." The process of intellectualization shows that certain forms of conflict solution may involve biological guarantees of an adaptation to external reality. It is well known that gratification, frustration, conflict, and anxiety, in optimal degree, are necessary for stimulating mental development from birth on. Detailed studies have demonstrated that too much or too little gratification, frustration, or anxiety beyond the optimum range on either end of the spectrum has a deleterious effect on intellectual development (115).

The term "learning" has neither a one-dimensional definition such as "acquiring data that becomes memory able to be recalled"; nor a one level of functioning such as conscious thinking. Not independent of other facets of mental development, learning is part of the overall mental growth which has been directly or indirectly influenced by events from embryo stages through independent life. Although difficult to precisely define, we know that volitional learning for survival, later for academic ends, evolves from a widely, distributed complicated network of brain cells that react to input stimulation starting even in embryonic life. The Nobel Prize in Medicine for year 2000 was awarded to three researchers who demonstrated that developmental experiences during the mother's pregnancy produced changes in communication receptor "memory cells" that enabled the storing of data which will be integrated and utilized, as in "learning." How a mass of primal neurones, the brain cells, becomes organized into a sophisticated learning function is a principal interest of many researchers from related scientific disciplines. A convergence of their studies suggests that learning develops from an instinct base (29,43,44,46,80).

What is an instinct?

Studied extensively in man, other vertebrates, and birds, an instinct has been defined as an unlearned pre-determined, probably genetically transmitted, survival reflex-mechanism present at birth. Most biologists agree that lower forms of living animals are better equipped than man to survive at birth. Animals at the upper end of the evolutionary scale, such as humans and great apes, need more and longer external support in obtaining food and physical protection than those at lower levels. The kangaroo baby "instinctively" and almost immediately, heads for milk, warmth, and food in its mother's pouch. The human neonate left to itself at birth, cannot eat, drink, or get warm "instinctively," and would soon perish from starvation, dehydration, and cold. The human neonates must acquire many of their adaptive, survival behaviors through learning. The emphasis on learning is translated into considerations about what experiences are appropriate; what frequency, intensity, and timing of them are likely to facilitate learning; what kind of encounters with specific people will enhance development. A mix between frustration and satisfaction is not only inevitable but desirable in the development of personality, but the balance should be favorable. "What is favorable?" has no objective answer other than "not excessive in frustration or pain; with more satisfactions than denials." Anna Freud quipped "Anxiety in appropriate intensity makes humans intelligent."

Instinct reactions occur between a stimulus called an external release stimulus (ERS) and responses to it called internal release responses (IRR). A popular example reported by Konrad Lorenz (64) is that of the newly hatched duckling attaching to him by an IRR to Lorenz's voice, the first sound the duckling heard. It is as if he were the mother calling via an ERS. Salk's (92) claim that mothers' heartbeats function as imprinting stimuli led him to place ticking clocks in bassinets to continue baby's bonding. Certainly a logical application to an unproven but informed allegation.

Reflex learning

Mother as the instinct

Put to the mother's chest but not directly to the breast, the human neonate does not try to suck. But if its cheek touches the breast, the rooting reflex turns the baby's head toward the stimulus. If the cheek touches the nipple, the baby will try to engulf it, but may need help in sucking. This rooting becomes modified very quickly and is one of the very few visible instinct behaviors in human babies. Repetitions of rooting are learning experiences; not volitional academic learning, but as labelled by Pavlov, "conditional reflex learning," as when a dog is conditioned and "learns" to salivate when a bell is sounded. When a hungry baby senses or sights the breast or bottle, or hears "mother" sounds and stops crying even though hunger was not appeased, that behavior indicates that a calming "conditional reflex learning" has occurred informin that "mother will come." This reflex response will underlie a personality trait at a later date called "confident expectation." Confidence that the mother will return with gratification proceeds to patience, the capacity to wait, and the control of impulses. The sight, sound, scent, and behavior of the mother as the "functioning instinct of the newborn" are imprinted into baby's memory cells which become survival structures created by the stimulations from the mothering figure.

Continuous stimulation-input creates a brain area, called the biological Ego, that will mirror and eventually replace the mother as "instinct" in baby's growth toward autonomy. Many behaviors-for-survival are stored in memory cells in the Ego through unending stimulus-response reflexes with the mother. The child's long period of dependence on her input ensures that she can communicate all that she, the first teacher, can teach. The importance of the quality, talent, responsiveness, and availability of the mothering figure as she prepares the child for independent life is self-evident (3,91).Repeated absences of the mother, even for short periods, will have long-term consequences. A baby's sense of time and an adult's sense of time do not measure absences by the same clock. At this crucial age of four to six months any absence is long for the ungratified infant. Absences can result in the caretaker, with whom the baby is left repeatedly, becoming the "mother" in the baby's memory.

Reflex responses, such as eyes following a bright light, or the functionally valuable rooting reflex, or the knee-jerk reflex suggest that some stimuli produce only an action response without mental tension intervening, as with hunger. This fact supports the hypothesis that "there is an innate instinctual response to the external world" which may be the biological basis for learning. An earlier, now discarded theory, had stated that the baby is just a passive recipient of stimulation imposed by the external world on the brain matter,and that the awareness of reality was created with further aging of higher centers of perception in the brain. But data such as the neonate turning toward, not away, from the breast and nipple forced reconsideration of the theory. In turning toward a stimulus the infant was considered to be actively seeking and responding to the external world within the limits of its maturational capacity to do so. This reaction is not just passive reception.

Current learning theory

Learning theory, always in flux from new data, states that in the creation of the ability to consciously and volitionally learn, innate reflex responses became conditioned by internal and external stimulations of brain cells. The primary components to reflex learning, the bedrock of all learning, are the baby's responses to strong enough yet not painful external stimuli that result in its turning toward the stimulus, rather than away from it. Maturation eventually leads to awareness and curiosity about external reality. The mental functions which effect the development of "people awareness," and "people relatedness," influence all learning just as they influence personality development.

Early, postnatal signs of learning (91,101,102)

The normal infant's urge to learn is readily recognized after the first three months of life. Normal babies explore the body-self, and their control of body and muscle skills that master the environment. Many isolated easily observable activities fit into learning about the world. A two-year-old putting pegs into holes is absorbed with learning the reality of the holes, the pegs, and the way to integrate these two realities into functional relationships. Mother and child learn clues from each other through a system of private and complicated preverbal communications that require prolonged observation. Non-verbal communication is the forerunner to the language of babbling, verbalization and speech (3,12,65). Roughly for the next few years when maturation enables the acquisition of symbols, conscious volitional learning proceeds at a rate probably never to be equalled in later life. "The essence of learning is the process of abstraction, of conceptualization, with the brain functions utilizing a sublimated form of energy. Regressions, when they occur, revive sexual and aggressive modes of energy, predisposing to learning problems" (13).

Learning structure

Academic learning does not evolve from a precise location in the brain, like sight or speech, but from a widely distributed complicated mosaic of developing mental functions that will grasp, integrate, and utilize subject matter. Many mental functions become organized in a psychological configuration, or structure that we can label as the "learning structure." This expands in a personalized fashion throughout life. Maturation leads to awareness of the total environment, progressing to curiosity, communication and abstract thinking.

This mental neurological structure can be disabled at any moment. Influences inimical to healthy maturation ranging from genetic defects, organic brain damage at birth, developmental deficits, acquired illnesses, tissue injuries, nutritional deficits, to inept parenting, and a myriad of other disruptive experiences in life may occur from the time of conception. This would account for the many forms and degrees of learning disabilities. It seems to be a biological principle that an earlier, less matured form more resistant to trauma, takes over automatically to provide as best it can the impaired function (9) when the healthy progressive development of a function is impaired.

A statistic about the incidence of learning problems

An increasing number of children have been referred to child psychiatrists and psychoanalysts for consultation for academic difficulties since 1930. In 1987 the United States Department of Education issued a report stating that 4.7%, or 1.9 million, of all public school-age children in the U.S. were receiving special education services for learning disabilities. That figure was actually lower than the actual number because children in private schools and private remediation were excluded for the poll (63,77). Teachers and psychologists in school systems had noted a special rejection learning-behavior in certain kindergarten and first-grade children. On entering school these children, from a broad spectrum of social and economic levels, seemed to lack any interest in learning. Instead of wanting "to become smart," as most cohorts do, they, were interested only in immediate gratification of impulses and desires and avoided learning academic skills by playing and fighting in class. This syndrome has been of special concern in Jamaica, where the overall incidence of illiteracy with it diverse degrees and forms of expression is estimated at 60 to 70 percent of the population.

"Woman smarter than man"

In the 1960s the physician in charge of pediatrics at Jamaica's University of The West Indies had noted that after surviving their first years of nutritional deprivations and usual childhood illnesses, Jamaican boy and girl babies developed into charming and alert two-and three-year-olds. At five and six years of age a dramatic difference in behavior between the sexes appeared. Many Jamaican children, but boys in particular, became unruly and disinterested in learning. Even though their testing revealed normal intelligence and general good health, they were uneducable and could not be taught written language, reading, or grammatical speech. First-graders showing indiscipline and refusal to learn were sent to the "doctor for injections," threatening that going to the doctor could be punishment.

Most age-similar girls on the other hand, were educable, surpassing the boys in academic achievement. Boys could be taught skills by practical demonstration of how something was to be done, but could not understand written or verbal instruction. Gender difference in behavior persisted throughout the years and influenced the employment market. The calypso song, "Woman Smarter Than Man" exemplified the fact no-one seemed to doubt. How did "woman become smarter than man in every way" was a challenging, but interesting question. A quick answer that this was the result of poor educational methods would have been banal, incomplete, and only an undocumented opinion. A valid answer to the question required that previously researched and reported causes of childhood learning impairments over the world be supplemented with local observations and individual diagnostic assessments. Developmental factors that predispose to different forms of learning difficulties are known. What known factors in the lives of Jamaican boys brings about the learning problem that makes them less educable relative to girls? The path to follow for answers to "why woman smarter?" starts with the earliest learning experiences with the mother figure.

Parents participate in the creation of psychologically based learning difficulties. Inappropriate interactions between neonate and mother may delay the appearance of the smile response, infant's desire to be held, to grasp, to touch, which are the first social contacts. Mother and child learn clues from each other through their own private language of non-verbal communication, the forerunner to verbalization and speech

(3,12,65). The quality of the mother's responses to the preverbal signals may promote or delay development of vocalization and babbling which are necessary for later speech and reading, Lack of stimulation, as well as unrelieved pain or frustration, are the rule for infants whose mothers can't "read them."

Definition of learning problems

Learning problems, the most frequent reason for child referral, had been diagnosed during the 1940s as Dyslexia, Hypermotility, or Attention Deficit Syndromes. These were classed among Minimal Brain Damage conditions characterized by "soft, yet pathological" neurological signs due to impaired development of neural pathways.Agreement about non-organic causations was limited and controversial.

However, ongoing research established a variety of diagnostic categories citing Organic, Genetic, Psychotic, and Neurotic causative factors grouped under two headings: one, organic substrate causation; two, psychological causation.Illiteracy, an inability or difficulty to grammatically read, write, speak, or comprehend is called complete; or, if the ability is present to read or write, but below grade level, with an impairment of comprehension the illiteracy is called partial; a limited ability to comprehend written, read, or verbalized information is called functional illiteracy.(75) Learning Disability is now identified as a group of behavioral syndromes with varied causations that present as illiteracy.

Evaluated both as an educational phenomenon and a psychiatric symptom, learning disability has an extensive research and clinical bibliography. As an educational phenomenon, learning difficulty, an inadequacy in scholastic achievement, is identified by a report card which measures the individual against an academic norm established by a local Board of Education. Modifying the norm, the expected standard of performance in the school, upwards or downwards alters the meaning of the report card without influencing or identifying the mental functions used for learning.

As a psychiatric symptom, a learning difficulty is a sign of functional impairment measured by a biological norm. The norms, determined for each age group by clinical observations and psychological tests on a vast cohort of children, are the timetable for predictable and expectable functioning for various age groups to be achieved. Child psychologists and educators now regard most children who have learning difficulties as suffering from psychiatric disturbances that warrant consultations.

Neurotic or emotional conflicts conflicts have been shown to not only impair but may also enhance artistic, musical, and mechanical abilities as well as academic skills. Precocity, which is an over-performance of function appearing before expected ages or maturational phases, is related to learning disorder. However, parents and teachers consider precocity or very early maturation, the gifted child, as a desirable deviation from the norm (13), Gifted children also require special educational measures to nurture and maintain their performance.

Physical and psychological developmental landmarks, beginning with the neonatal days, are manifestations of a developmental timetable that are obtained through accurate data-gathering over years. They offer insights into the health of a baby's development, the normality of behavioral expressions, and assist in the refining of assessments and diagnoses. Landmarks are used as "signs" in determining whether various functions are developing in a healthy or retarded manner. With an understanding of their genesis and meaning, many diagnostic questions can be investigated and future development predicted.

For example, the "smile response landmark reveals important information about the progress of the child's mental development. What does it mean when a baby at two or three months age smiles indiscriminately at any bobbing head? What does it mean if baby doesn't smile at the same stimulus at six months later? What if the baby cries at sight of many heads from four to six months and only smiles at particular "heads"? These questions are as important as "does baby crawl, turn over, stand, talk, as expected at various ages" that most pediatricians will ask a parent. The presence or absence of various physical landmarks at expectable ages point to healthy or impaired development. The same applies to psychological landmarks of which there are many. The "smile reflex" may be examined as a model of the many.

A landmark: smile reflex

In human maturation and development, the awareness of the external world arises before its separateness from the baby's inside-reality of imagery and feelings is comprehended by the baby. Up until the latter part of the second month the psyche or mind is a primeval fog of external and internal stimuli, undifferentiated and not distinguished by the baby as to source or aim inside or outside the body. The self is the baby's world. Then a remarkable and basic transformation begins at about three months heralded by the "smile reflex." If an observer introduces his head into a baby's line of vision before baby is three months old nothing of note occurs. Then at about three months a remarkable event takes place.If the observer now nods his head the baby will smile. Parents say "see the baby knows me" or others may add "no,it's gas." Neither is true. Any bobbing head, or even a balloon with eyebrows painted on it, causes a reflexive smile. The baby is responding to an external stimulus, a Gestalt, that announces that inside and outside perceptions are being differentiated and a healthy development is in progress. The infant now recognizes the "outside reality" as separate from "the inside." The reflex reveals changes with maturation that is the beginning of the conscious differentiation of the world of reality from fantasy. Many babies who will later be psychotic, autistic children, do not show that landmark.

As the next three or four months pass, the smile reflex changes its reaction and is joined by "head and eye" following of moving objects in the external environment. The smile reflex is reserved for the caretaker or mother's face that the child now recognizes by sight as well as by body scent, sound, and touch. When a different face appears the child may cry inconsolably until the constant figure, mother or caretaker, reappears. This reaction signifies the baby's recognition, or differentiation from a number of faces, that "This face is my/not my caretaker," underlining the importance of the constancy of presence of that known "face" for recognition. Grandparents are often disappointed when the child cries at them! But this is in fact a sign of baby's healthy mental development. At about six months of age the baby will recognize more "faces" but will cry at "strangers." Related to an earlier separation fear when mother was not seen, at this time it is the normal, expected beginning of "stranger anxiety." The intensity of stranger anxiety reaction varies from child to child and remains through life, though on a decreasing level of intensity. If an intense stranger anxiety remains into the child's fifteenth month it may portend a later paranoia. If it has been absent, it may indicate a child who will be vulnerable to danger.

The relationship to a constant "mother" is all important. If her absence, felt by the baby as loss or abandonment, produces the inconsolable reaction, falling asleep may be impaired, pre-school attendance may not be achieved, and eating disturbances may appear. Anaclitic depression is a severe result of the loss of the dependent that has been established during the first six months to mother or caretaker. If that person is removed by death, divorce, or abandonment the baby will not accept a substitute as compensation and will refuse food and comfort. Some mothers feeling jealous of the baby's attachment to a caretaker and angered by the baby crying at mother, may dismiss the caretaker and thereby aggravate the baby's reaction to loss.If the person is able to return in time, the consequence, if it has not reached the catastrophic state, will improve. If she does not return in time, the baby may continue a down ward course to an irreversible physical and psychological retardation.

Hospitalized, abandoned babies follow a similar course and often develop a condition called marasmus, an irreversible physical and psychological starvation picture. These and other separations from the mother that have caused psychological developmental retardations have been classified as "Psychogenic Diseases of Early Childhood" (102) and lead to learning disorders. Adopted children, represent at least 2% of the population, and probably unreported adoptions add more. Yet, census reports from mental hygiene services, the educational realm, and international records report 15% of adopted children were in remedial education services. Recent Swedish studies testify to this over-representation of adopted children with learning problems, as do Danish and English reports.These childrens show problems that are related to the fact of having been told of their relinquishment, they say "gotten rid of," and therefore separated from their mother.

Fear of sleep, strange food habits are among other consequences to prolonged separations. Dependence on and attachment to inanimate "fetish" objects, such as blankets, diapers, soothers, normally symbols for the mother, may develop in children whose mothers are "more or less" present but whose absences contribute tension and longing in the baby. As transient phenomena these attachments are in fact aids to the infant's mastery of separation fears, until further development allows for psychological solutions.

The term "symbiotic relationship" describes a normal, overdependent relationship that exists between a mother and child from ages 12 to 24 months when both are prisoners of each other. They seem unable to live with or without each other. If it continues unabated over dependence disables the development of childhood speech functions important for academic learning. Mother and child, as a dyad, understand each other by gestures, or at times with only a sound, making fulfillment of wishes via a secret communication possible. When the symbiotic relationship extends beyond three years, it becomes a disability in the development of independent functioning, which includes learning academically.

A too common behavioral symptom of retained symbiosis seen in Jamaican medical facilities is best defined anecdotally. A mother may come into the doctor's office to talk about her child's illness. "How old is your child?" she is asked. "Twenty two," she may reply. When the "child" comes in and is asked, "What is wrong?" he will turn to his mother instead of answering, waiting for her to talk for him. She replies to the examiner, "I told you already!" If the child were ten or less he might crawl up into the mother's lap and grope to retrieve her breast, treating her body as his own, and the mother will act as if nothing unusual is happening

Crying is an all or none response to many sources of a neonate's distress. Eventually it becomes a controlled, many-toned communication between mother and infant. They learn to distinguish between causes of the distress through the nuances of the baby sounds and the responses by mother. Further maturation into vocalization and babbling, the precursors of later speech, the source of the term "mother tongue," and reading may be promoted or delayed by the mother's responses. Inappropriate interaction by the mother and other adults may thwart an infant's need to being held to "melt" or mold to the mother's body. These expressions of early social contacts are necessary factors for later academic learning as well. The presence of these reactions mean development is progressing. If they do not appear, troubled learning may be expected in the future.

School performance

Educators know the futility of trying to teach certain academic skills before particular mental functions have developed. The abilities to learn to read, write, and do arithmetic, as examples, emerge as part of a maturational timetable. At certain ages, therefore, many children may not yet be equipped with the needed functions. Forcing children to learn prematurely can exaggerate developmental and emotional conflicts which further interfere with future learning. All studies of children at risk of impaired development report the vulnerability of children to absent or ruptured meaningful family units. Provence, (22.p 582.) states, "I will begin by assuming the family remains the setting of choice for rearing infants in this country, though I realize some will question this. That some families are noxious and destructive for infants, that some are unable to provide a healthy child-rearing environment in today's complex and stressful world, that many need assistance on a scale not now available, that our current methods are often too little and too late, I accept as a reality. However, these factors do not, it seems to me, argue against the probability that a family unit is likely to remain the most important and constructive place in which to rear children, given the high value we continue to place upon individual development and upon resourcefulness and creativity. Increasingly there may be family groups of nonrelatives in which members assume roles and make abiding commitments to one another of sufficient strength and continuity that they are able to function well as child-rearing environments. Such groups would simulate a family in the protectiveness, dynamic importance of its members to each other, and the support systems for adults and children provided by a well functioning, traditional family."

Despite verbalized concern over illiteracy in Jamaica very little research into its prevalence has been scientifically explored there. An appalling statement from Jamaica's Ministry of Education about plans to "ban illiteracy in two years" revealed unrealistic concepts of the problem and cure. Naivete about the multifold causes of the problem to be "banned," and a militant political zeal uncooled by insights that basic scientific knowledge brings, produced a "political" promise that is unfulfillable. As a mix of numerous causes each learning disability must first be assessed. No mass, single-minded program based on an assumed one cause country-wide illiteracy will help.How can maturational delays, psychiatric disablements, and culturally determined disabilities be forced "to learn."

Latency

Educators had empirically decided that the optimum time to begin most childrens' academic learning was at five or six years of age. Psychological studies of stages of childhood confirmed this wisdom by showing that academic learning can only proceed with desexualized and deaggressivized, or neutralized, mental energies. Raw, early childhood sexual and aggressive energies, whose existence the world has such trouble acknowledging, must be modified in their aims and neutralized through mental functions that include sublimation. This neutralization process starting at four or five years of age heralds the development of a phase of childhood preceding pre-adolescence called the "Latency Period." Through the parental communication of required cultural, social behavior and the consequences of transgressions, controls of sexual and aggressive impulses become more stable. Qualities of personality that inhibit immediate gratifications develop. If latency progresses inadequately sexual curiosity will not be transformed into non-sexual curiosity of the world but will remain sexual curiosity seeking direct gratification (11). Curiosity of the world and academic learning utilize only desexualized and deaggressivized energies. The slow, hard work of learning and socializing are experienced by learning-disabled children as interferences with pleasure-seeking and are therefore avoided with parental collusion. In this simple context the role of parents in nurturing learning disabilities of a non-organically produced type is explained.

Developmental givens possessed by all children

Children the world over are born with the same biological givens, but their characters and personalities develop at different rates and directions according to cultural and parental influences. Maldevelopment will take many and varied forms, such as illiteracy, or delinquency, or drug abuse, even suicide. In sifting the information about these "problems," and in fact for any behavioral problems, data relating to early adverse influences on childhood development for each problem always emerge. The question "What known factors in the lives of the Jamaican boys," for example, "bring about the learning problem that makes them ineducable relative to girls?" should be rephrased to, "What factors lead to drug use, suicide, or violence, or any other malfunctioning in young people?" The path to follow for answers always begins with the history of the earliest experiences with the mothering figure from babyhood and childhood.

The special influences of parents and grandparents through ther handed-down myths and superstitions that perpetuate culturally determined child-rearing practices throughout the world, are detailed in volumes of scientific literature. Parents emphasize that their home life is governed by a "love of children" and in accordance with psychology's recommendations for successful emotional development. A closer look at the histories, however, usually reveals two areas of question. Infantile finger sucking, infantile masturbation, sexual curiosity, or exhibitionism were allowed unrestricted expression; and children had been permitted to operate always on the principle of immediate gratification of impulses and desires.

Parents frequently and unwisely protect children from any emotional pain occasioned by normal and necessary frustrations in life. Children raised with parental misunderstanding of the degree of permissiveness recommended by psychologists, will not tolerate anxiety or anger. The development of those mental functions of the personality that change raw infantile sexuality and aggression into a neutral form may become severely retarded. The children so affected cannot control their hostile aggressive impulses which arise when immediate gratification of impulses or desire is prevented or delayed by reality. They react with anger and fear to the slow, difficult acquisition of skills necessary for learning and independent living. In situations of arrested development, the symbiotic dependence on the mother is sustained into the child's own parenthood and passed to succeeding generations via behavior.

There are numerous other ways that parents participate in the creation of non-organically caused behavioral symptoms. As examples, conflicting beliefs about the "value" of boys compared to girls in the culture are potent influences on character formation; many children are "spoiled" by elders in the family who create a double standard for behavior where boys can, girls can't. "Little girls don't urinate at will against a tree; a boy may grope the mother's body as if it were his own" stimulating his raw sexual urges repeatedly. Academic education is not always considered necessary and children will be taught and are expected to learn what the numerous ethnic communities believe to be important. Girls achieve the controls necessary for social behavior and benefit from the restraints that boys had not incurred. At times child-rearing practices contribute to "Woman Smarter," and boys illiteracy.

There are individual differences in parents' readiness for parenthood and their capacity to function. An infant's characteristic of changing needs and behavioral style always affect parental attitudes and behavior.

Just as growing up is fraught with developmental crises and adaptations for the child, adults experience parenting as adifficult adaptation and developmental experience. Along with its gratifications, child rearing is a stressful task for which most parents need psychological and tangible supports from their own families, or from professionals, or some community resource. To develop as parents and nurture the child in a healthy way, it is fair to assume that the teenage parent is the most in need.

It is not always easy, even for the skilled professional, to understand the caretaker in the role of parent. A parent prefers to see him/herself as an independent individual, instead of as a participant, not as an active contributor to the satisfactions or frustrations of a child at different ages in a family unit. Failure to see themselves in a "functional unit" will impede development of the infant. This is of special importance since parents themselves usually only see the child as the "problem."

Treatment (75,76)

"The professional help for the learning disabled comes from tutors. Tutoring would hardly appear to need definition, let alone description. As a term it is so easily comprehended, so self-illuminating, it seems to define itself. Yet it has not found its way into any comprehensive dictionary of psychological terms. In practice, however, tutoring has become a specific technique within the complex proliferation of educational specialties." There are varying gradations sophistication and professionalism of techniques in tutoring, ranging from short-term preparation of the well integrated, well motivated student who requires services of a subject-expert tutor for a temporary and specific effort, to long-range remedial efforts. The latter may span crucial stages of development and even act as a major psychological influence for psychotherapeutic intervention (75).

Tutors are educational specialists in learning disability. They tend to polarize around two main theoretical foundations concerned with significant etiological factors. One group emphasizes behavioral modifications, while the other stresses dynamic psychological considerations. The behavioral remedial tutors relate learning disability to neurological, perceptual, and physiological factors as in dyslexia, language disability, minimal brain damage, and developmental lags. This approach stresses clearly circumscribed instruction and training-retraining techniques.

At the other pole are the specialists who define the dynamics of the dysfunction as it relates to the child's psychological development. They see learning disability as a symptom of inhibition in an emotional conflict. It is perhaps more fruitful to adopt a simple axiom that learning failure is multidetermined. Tutoring then is considered by the second group as an adjunct, almost a clone, of psychotherapeutic technique.

The tutorial situation is essentially one of relationship. The tutor hopes for, but should not expect, a traditional student-teacher relationship as with a compliant, docile, and responsive pupil, and friendly cooperative parents. Children and parents carry an unrealistic stereotype image of the tutor.Interviews with parents often start out with their denials of any emotional problems of their child and see the tutor as a quick dispenser of help for learning. In their minds the tutor will give instruction and the child will passively or magically absorb it. They view tutoring as something given and the tutor a hired instrument. In a sense they want the child to see the tutor as a taskmaster, a drill sergeant. It doesn't work that way. Many parents, because they are embarrassed by the child's failure, quickly turn to tutoring to avoid the recognition of deeper problems in the child.

As a rule children do not welcome being tutored at first, indeed for some it is painful. Disabled children cannot sustain attention in formalized structures, such as in a group or class. Yet children with organic problems need a structure, but not of the traditional type. The structure evolves from the tutor-student relationship.

The tutorial relationship is a complex interactive process where basically the teacher and student vacillate between the tutor's active "giving" and passive "listening" to the pupil, who must actively "take in" and passively "listen" to the tutor. The child comes to perceive the tutor as a constant, significant person who responds to his/her needs. The tutor by making demands for learning within a relationship of acceptance affords the child open avenues for independence and self assertion. A child who learns to read after the frustrating periods of failure will perceive the experience as a palliative to the pain of humiliation. The object of tutoring, as with psychotherapy, is to enable a child to function. Each child must be evaluated and the relationship modified according to the child's unique capabilities and circumstance.

Apropos of treatment without proper assessment, parents of children treated with Ritalin for AD/HD (attention deficit and hypermotility disorder that interfered with school learning) are suing Novartis, the manufacturer, and the American Psychiatric Association for collusion to increase sales of Ritalin. Whether or not the children had developed their needed functions had not been diagnosed 40 years ago. Did premature and long-term medicating prevent the normal development of those functions needed to prevent the problem? The question of "What is the overall effect of long term-medication on developing mental structures?" is still unaddressed.

Epilogue

A person is an awesomely complex totality. So many complexities and all in one package. No one is capable of studying and understanding Man all in one piece and all at once. So we break up the study of Man into more manageable fragments such as biology, psychology, anthropology, sociology. As the study of Man becomes more specialized and fragmented, the specialists lose touch with each other. When they make contact again, they usually do battle. Mind versus body and genetic inheritance versus environment are two of the better known controversies.

But mind and body, genetic inheritance and environment are Man-made pigeonholes. They are not the separate and distinct entities we once thought. Man himself is the distinct entity divided up by the disciplines that study him. So it is futile to believe that the solution to the problems being considered, along with any others, will be achieved by single-minded emphasis on any one discipline. Biomedical or anthropological or economic or sociological studies separately will not supply the answers. We have to put it all together.

The psychological viewpoint is the glue that puts it all together and places the "drug problem," for example, in new and proper perspective. Terminology and formulations based on the psychological facts of life enabled us to penetrate more deeply into causes of drug abuse as pathological exaggerations of some aspects of normal human behavior. We may assert that drug abuse is only one of many forms of disturbance, and not a new "epidemic" disease to which all adolescents will succumb. From our vantage point we then attempt reasonable answers to: "Why doesn't everyone abusively use drugs? When does normal use become abnormal?" Emphasis of psychological factors may supply some answers but not the solutions. Nor can biomedical or anthropological or economic or sociological studies separately supply the solutions.

Extracted from my own professional activities and a vast bibliography, this presentation is an abridged version of crucial areas in the genesis of particular problems. It attempts only to offer interested readers a valid answer to the introductory question of, "Why, after all the time and money that has been spent, have these knotty problems not been loosened, even if not unraveled?" Highlighted in the histories, ambiguous terminology and definitions stand out as indisputably resulting in the creation of invalid theories. Clinical inexperience of the planners compounded their conceptual errors, and augmented by the force of political expediency abetted by media misrepresentations allowed laymen to derail scientific study. Antagonism to basic psychological data and monotonous repetitious resurrection of worn-out theories and failed programs are important visible factors in failures. The absence of adequately trained personnel to plan or initiate strategies is central to the billions of dollars wasted on these scattered non-performing programs, and should have been be rectified before implementation.

These factors contributing to the failure of the programs waging "war" on drugs, illiteracy, and adolescent disturbances should be considered as the many, regenerating heads of the Hydra, that will not be successfully attacked individually as "basic causes." The search for "basic causes" of each problem is an effort of futility and denial as long as consequences are considered the causes. The "hydra's immortal head," ulimately the basic cause, are the early disturbances in healthy childhood development, and applies to many programs that deal with reform of the human animal. The head should be attacked directly as the important basic cause of malfunction in general.

The question then always arises "What should we do?" But to present a strategy on "What to do for solution," as if I must have one, was not intended. Just because I criticize the programs doesn't mean I must supply another useless theory or that we must keep the failures! So the question is inappropriate. I have no magic with which to supply mass cures for these ills, and, as stated, it is inconceivable that any single-minded emphasis of any one relevant discipline will unravel the puzzle of society's malfunctioning. To offer one at this point in time, therefore, would amount to my joining the crowd offering unrealistic opinions. I say let's look first. I believe we can only comprehend the complexity of the problems if reviews of the history of drug abuse, adolescent indiscipline, and illiteracy are integrated into the discussion of why programs failed. And enable an avoidance of these pitfalls, if we can, in future planning!

To explain how or why something went on wrong "basically" in human behavior, whether on an individual or community level, normal development and its obstacles should first be known to the reformers. It is the author's opinion that by not acknowledging relevant historical background, the programmers "programmed for failure." The failed programs themselves confirm we are off on the wrong path. To repeat, flawed programs derive from flawed theories which had not been critically examined by the new planners.

Before any solutions are even proposed, all statistics, proposals, claims, and counterclaims should be reviewed from unified realistic definitions, empirical data, and underlying theories. From the mass of existing information, formulations upgraded by modern concepts could tentatively initiate a common language to prevent Babel. To begin to neutralize the Hydra's head I can suggest two lines of approach that may seem naieve about the topic of "money," and pessimistically about man's readiness to change his false beliefs.

One, which will be controversial at its proposal, is: form a Think Tank of professionally respected, informed representatives of relevant disciplines chaired by an experienced psychoanalyst, to integrate the diverse data and offer new formulations from this unique investigatory point of view. In other words find out what we know, not what we think we know. We are less in need of more data and theories than of a systematic examination of what is already available. New discovery is certainly valuable; and for many rediscovery is educational and confirmatory of established data. But it can also become an endless review of failed projects and theories.

The second proposal would be to create a proper research staff that could go into homes to study the quality and content of existing child-rearing practices and the mother-child reactions that occur. This of course would require shifting funds from the unproductive "clean up the mess" programs to the needed numbers of participating investigators. The study would really be taking aim on the Hydra's head. Hopefully the causal factors of impairments to early childhood development beginning from the neonatal days could be influenced. Although this would require an expanded infrastructure for the education and monitoring of staff activities, the cost of the time of sober reflection would be the least expensive for potentially rich results, and the most innovative approach in the long run (71).

Considering the vast amount of money wasted on a variety of "failing, clean up the mess programs," the stopping of these worthless programs would be no loss. The use of those funds, and possibly more, to finance mothers who, for example, must work or follow careers but should remain with their children in the first year of life at least would be more than justified. The transitory absences of the mother/father for even important reasons, such as to have careers or earn a living, during the first two years of the baby's life can be inimical to healthy development. The government should finance the mothers and fathers for extended maternity leaves. Government should expand financial participation into the workplace by developing day-care facilities with proper supervisors to increase the time for parental presence, bonding, and guidance.

Such a proposal will immediately be criticized as unrealistic and expensive. But expensive, wasteful, unrealistic programs are already in existence and should be stopped. Denmark, Norway, and Sweden have seen the wisdom of similar suggested approaches, and despite opposition from a number of sources including some parents themselves, have already inaugurated related programs to keep families intact. If the governments or public resist such proposals, a change in their priorities of importance from "money relations to human relations" would be another project.

About the Author

Dr. Herbert Wieder is a graduate of the New York University-Bellevue Hospital College of Medicine in New York City, and of the New York Psychoanalytic Institute. He has served on the medical faculties of New York University College of Medicine, Albert Einstein College of Medicine, and Downstate Medical School (SUNY).

A Life Member of the American Psychoanalytic Association, the American Psychiatric Association, the International Psychoanalytic Association, and Child Analysis Association, he is a past president of the Long Island Psychoanalytic Society. Certified since 1955 as a psychoanalyst for adults, he holds additional certification for specializing in children and adolescents. He founded and directed the Adoption Study Center at Brookdale Hospital Medical Center in 1978. This facility was the first and only research unit affiliated with a major medical institution in the United States studying the lives of adoptive families, which he wrote about in a book "Handbook on Adoption" aimed for the general public. His scientific papers have been translated for the first volume in a series on adoption published by the Hamburg Psychoanalytic Society in Germany. In 1946, early in his career, Dr. Wieder was part of the original research team evaluating Methadone and other drugs at the United States Public Health Service Hospital at Lexington Kentucky where he was in charge of the admission and withdrawal service.

His many contributions to the scientific literature are published in the prestigious Journals of The American Medical Association, The Journal of the American Psychoanalytic Association, The Psychoanalytic Quarterly, and The Journal of Nervous and Mental Diseases. His studies have been included in the Psychoanalytic Study of the Child and other scientific volumes. Centered around the development of drug abuse theory and treatment, he authored a book "Drugs Dont Take People" with a colleague, Dr. Eugene H. Kaplan. Intellectuality, early childhood learning theory, drug use in adolescence, and adoption issues have been the range of his professional studies initiated by clinical work in the problems of the young.

Currently Dr. Wieder practices in Jamaica, West Indies where he had been a consultant in the Ministry of Health and had worked at the University of the West Indies in the Department of Pediatrics. He had also been on the out-patient staff at the St.Ann's Bay Hospital for 20 years, and had been a member of the Jamaican National Council on Drug Abuse. He lives with his artist wife, Jonna Brasch, at Anancy's Web, their home on the Caribbean sea.

Bibliography

1. Aichorn,A. (1948) Wayward Youth Viking Press New York.

2. Aries, P. (1962) The psychology of adolescence (in Esman 18, p.3)

3. Balint, A. (1954) The Early Years of Life Basic Books New York

4. Batterman, R. C., and Himmelsbach, C. K. (1946) Demerol: A New Synthetic Analgesic A Review Of Its Present Status and Comparison With Morphine. JAMA pp. 222-226 May 22 .

5. Bender. L. Keiser, S. Schilder, P. (1936) Studies in aggression, from Bellevue Hospital, Psychiatric Division and Medical College of New York University. Monograph 18:357-564.

6. Bender, L. and Schilder, P. (1937) Suicidal preoccupations and attempts in children A.J.Orthopsy. 7:225-234.

7. Bernfeld, S. (1923) Uber eine typische Form der mannliche Pubertat Imago 9

8.—(1938) Types of adolescence Psa.Quart 7:243-253

9. Blanchard, P. (1936) Psychoanalytic contributions to the problem of reading disabilities PsaStCh: vol 2. IUP NY

10. Blos, P. (1967) The second individuation process of adolescence PsaStCh. 22:162-186 IUP NY

11. Bornstein, B. (1951) On latency PsaStCh. 6: 279-285. IUP NY

12. Bowlby,J.(1951) Maternal care and mental health Geneva WHO

13. Buxbaum, E. (1964) The role of parents in the etiology of learning disabilities PsaStCh.19: 421-427. IUP NY

14. Carroll, Lewis (1880) The walrus and the carpenter from: Through the Looking Glass and What Alice Saw.

15. Catlin, G. (1973) Letters and notes on the manners, customs and conditions of the North American Indians 2 vols. Dover publications NY

16. Daunton, E. (1978) The nursery school as an accompaniment to psychoanalysis, Child Analysis and Therapy 529-554 Aronson NY

17. Conferences On Drug Addiction Among Adolescents 1952 The New York Academy of Medicine Blakiston Company New York Nov. 30 March

18. Deutsch,H. (1967) Selected problems of adolescence. IUP NY

19. Dole, V. P. and Nyswander, M. A. (1965) A Medical Treatment of Diacetyl Morphine (Heroin) Addiction: A Clinical Trial With Methadone JAMA 1938 646-650.

20. Dole, V. P. and Nyswander, M. A. (1965) Methadone Maintenance and its implication for theories of narcotic addiction. Assoc. for Research in Nervous and Mental Diseases 46: 359-366.

21. Eissler, K. (1958) Notes on problems of technique in the psychoanalytic treatment of adolescents: with some remarks on perversions. Psa. St. Child 13: 223-254 IUP NY

22. Esman, A. (1975) Editor Psychology of Adolescence IUP NY

23. Emerson, H. (1953) Conferences On Drug Addiction Among Adolescents New York Academy of Medicine Vol.1 Blakiston NY

24. Encyclopaedia Britannica China Opium Wars pp. 528-529.

25. Erikson, E. (1968) Identity: Youth and Crisis Norton NY

26. Federation Against Drug Addiction (FADA) (1971) Magic Bullets to Immunize Against Addiction Brochure10.

27. Felix, H. (1939) Some comments on the psychopathology of drug addiction Mental Hygiene 23: 567-578.

28. Fraiberg, S. (1959) The Magic Years Scribner

29. Frazer, M.B. (1974) Strategies for the prevention of drug abuse in developing countries. March 3-5 Special reference to the Caribbean and the Bahamas. The Law and Cannabis in the West Indies

30. Freud, A. (1944) Infants without families IUP NY

31. Freud, A. (1966) The Ego and the Mechanisms of Defense IUP NY

32. Freud, A. (1965) Normality and pathology in childhood: assessments of development IUP NY.

33. Freud, S. Three Contributions to the Theory of Sex(1905) SE. 14: 67-258 Hogarth Press London

34. Freud, S. (1953) From the "Life And Works of Sigmund Freud" E. Jones vol 1 Basic Books.

35. Freud, S. (1926) Inhibition, symptoms and anxiety SE. XX p. 124 Hogarth Press.

36. Frosch, W. A. (1970) Psychoanalytic evaluation of addiction and habituation JAPsA.18: 208-219.

37. Glenn, J. (1978) Editor Child Analysis and Therapy Jason Aronson NY

38. Gould, R. E. (1971) Methadone Reconsidered: A Critical Appraisal of the Methadone Maintainence Program and Alternative Methods for the Treatment of Heroin Addiction. Drug Therapy pp.16-29 Aug. 1

39. Hartmann, D. (1969) A study of drug using adolescents. PsaStChild 24: 384-398 IUP NY

40. Himmelsbach, C. K. (1941) Morphine Abstinence Syndrome: Its Nature and Treatment, and Recovery. Ann.Internal Med.15:829-839 Nov.

41. Himmelsbach, C. K. (1941) Clinical Study of Drug Addiction: Physical Dependence, Withdrawal, and Recovery. Arch. Int. Med. 69: 766-772 May.

42. Howell, S. A. (1959) The Golden Age of Quackery MacMillan N. Y.

43. Hug-Hellmuth, H. (1920) Childhood psychology and education InJPsa 1: 316-323.

44. Inhelder, B., Piaget, J. (1958) The growth of logical thinking from childhood to adolescence Free Press.

45. Isbell, H. et al. (1947) Tolerance and Addiction Liability of Methadone JAMA 35: 885-894.

46. Isaacs, S. (1930) Intellectual growth in young children London George Ruttledge.

47. Jacobson, E. (1961) Adolescent moods and remodelling of the psychic structure in adolescence. Psa.St. Ch. 16:164-183.

48. Jones, R. T. (1971) New York Academy of Sciences: Conferences on Marijuana Reported in The Sciences 11: 21-22.

49. Kalinowski, L. B. (1943) Convulsions in Non-Epileptic Patients On Withdrawal From Drugs. Arch.Neurol Psych.48: 946-956 Dec.

50. Kaplan, E.H. and Wieder, H. (1974) Drugs Don't Take People Lyle Stuart Secausus N.J.

51. Kestenberg, J. S. (1967 and 1968) Phases of adolescence JAAcChPsy.6:426-463, 7:577-614.

52. Khantzian E. J. (1985) Self Medication Hypothesis of Addictive Disorders AJPsy vol.142#11 pp1259-1264 Nov.

53. Khantzian, E. J. et al. (1974) Heroin use as an attempt to cope: clinical observations AJPsy 131(2): 160-164.

54. Klee, G. (1963) LSD-25 and Ego Functions Arch. Gen. Psych 8: 461-474.

55. Kolb, L. (1938) Marijuana Federal Probation July.

56. Kolb, L., and Himmelsbach, C. K.(1938) Clinical Studies in Drug Addiction AJPsy.94: 4.

57. Kolb, L. and Himmelsbach, C. K. (1938) Drug Addiction:Clinical StudySupplement#128 Public Health Service Reports.

58. Kolb, L., and Ossenfort, W. F. (1935) The Treatment of Drug Addicts at the Lexington Hospital. SMedJ31:914-922 Aug.

59. Kramer, J. D. et al.(1967) Amphetamine Abuse: Patterns and Effects of High Doses Taken Intravenously JAMA 201: 305-309.

60. Lample-deGroot,J. (1960) On adolescence Psa.St.Ch. 15:95-103.

61. Laufer, M. (1965) Assessment of adolescent disturbance. Application of Anna Freud's Diagnostic profile Psa.St.CH. 20: 99-123.

62. Lester, R. Symposium (1971) On Alcoholism 5th World Congress of Psychiatry Mexico City.

63. Liss, E. (1949) Psychiatric implications of the failing student AJOrthopsy XIX

64. Lorenz, K. (1957) Companionship in birds (in) Instinctive Behavior Schiller IUP NY

65. Mahler, M. S. (1969) On Human Symbiosis and Vicissitudes of Individuation (with M. Furer) Vol. 1 Infantile Psychosis London Hogarth Press.

66. Mahler, M. S. (1963) Thoughts about development and individuation Psa.St.Ch:18: 307-324

67. Markham, J. M. (1972) Survey shows Methadone is joining Heroin on the blackmarket NY Times Jan 24.

68. Markham, J. M. (1972) Methadone rising as killer NY Times Mar 4.

69. Meade, M. (1961) Coming of age in Samoa (girls), and Growing up in New Guinea (boys) William Morrow Co. Inc. (in) Esman (21)

70. Merck (1899) Manual of Materia Medica Merck and Co.

71. National Institute on Drug Abuse (1977) Research Monograph 12: Psychodynamics of Drug Dependence May.

72. Nature Neuro-Science (2000) pp:799-806 Aug.

73. New York Narcotic Addiction Control Commission Survey. (1971) Psychiatric News 6: 17 Nov.

74. O'Malley, J. F. et al (1972) Failure of Outpatient Treatment of Heroin Drug Abuse AJPsy. 128: 865-868

75. Opperman, J. (1978) Tutoring: The remediation of cognitive and academic deficit by individual instruction. (in) Glenn (22) pp. 495-553.

76. Opperman,J. (1969) In : The theraputic nursery school editors R. Furman and A. Katan pp.274-292 IUP New York.

77. Pearson, G. (1952) A Survey of Learning Difficulties in ChildrenPsa.St.Ch. 7: 322-386.

78. Pescor, M. J. (1939) The Kolb Classification of Drug Addicts Supplement #155 Public Health Service Reports.

79. Pescor, M. J. (1943) Statistical Analysis Of The Clinical Records Of Hospitalized Drug Addicts Public Health Service Reports Supplement#143.

80. Piaget, J. (1945) Play, dreams, and imitation in childhood Norton

81. Psychiatric News (2000) Placebo response confounds drug trials July

82. Psychiatric News (1998) Psychotherapy Treatment Role Under Debate Feb.

83. Psychiatric News (1997) Methadone Treatment Reduces Harm Aug.

84. Psychiatric News (1997) Heroin Program in Switzerland Sept.

85. Psychiatric News (1998) Report recommends steps for increasing addiction research Feb.

86. Psychiatric News (1980) Nida to cosponsor special track on substance abuse Feb.

87. Rado, S. (1933) The Psychoanalysis of Pharmacothymia (drug addiction) 1. The clinical picture. Psychoan.Quart. #1: 1-23.

88. Rado, S. (1926) The Psychic Effects Of Intoxicants: an attempt to evolve a psychoanalytic theory of morbid cravings Int. Jour. Psa Vol 7: 396-413.

89. Rado, S. (1957) Narcotic Bondage: a general theory of dependence on narcotic drugs AJPsy. 114: 165-170.

90. Reichard, J. D (1947) Addiction: Some Theoretical Considerations As To Its Nature, Cause, Prevention, and Treatment AJPsy. 6 May.

91. Ribble, M. (1943) The rights of infants Columbia UP NY

92. Salk, L. (1962) Mother's heartbeat as an imprinting stimulus Transactions N.Y.Acad.Sci.Series ii Vol.24 no.7

93. Sakel, M. (1930) Theorie der Sucht Zeit. f.Gessam.Neuro, und Psy.139: 639

94. Savitt, R. (1963) Psychoanalytic studies on addiction Psa.Quart 32: 43-57.

95. Sears Roebuck Catalogue (1897) Chelsea House N. Y.

96. Services Research Monongraph Series National Drug/Alcohol collaborative project US. Dept. of Health, Education, and Welfare Alcohol, Drug Abuse, and Mental Health Adm. NIDA.

97. Shapiro, A. K. The Placebo Effect of Treatment Drug Therapy Vol. 1: 45-54.

98. Sigerest, H. E. A. (1967) A History of Medicine. Vol. 1 Primitive and Archaic Medicine Oxford University Press N.Y.

99. The Social Basis of Drug Abuse (Jacobson and Zinberg) (1975) Drug Abuse Council.

100. Spiegel, L. A. (1951) A review of contributions to a psychoanalytic theory of adolescence : individual aspects. Psa.St. Ch. 6:375-393.

101. Spitz,R. A. (1951) The psychogenic diseases in infancy Psa.St.Ch. 6

102. Spitz, R. A. (1965) The First Year of Life (with W.Godfrey Cobliner) IUP NY

103. Stone,L.J. and Church, J. Adolescence as a cultural invention (in) Esman (18) p.7

104. Tanner, J. M. (1962) Growth at adolescence 2nd. edition Oxford: Blackwell.

105. U. S. National Research Council (1995) "Rethink The War On Drugs and Crime" Internet May 5.

106. U. S. Treasury (1938) Department of Narcotics Opium and Coca Leaves Regulation #5 with Later Amendments June 1.

107. Welfare Council of New York City (1951): The Menace of Narcotics to the Children of New York: A plan to eradicate the evil Aug.

108. Wickler, A. A. (1952) A Psychodynamic Study of a Patient During Experimental Self-regulated Re-addiction to Morphine. Psych.Quart. 26:270-293.

109. Wickler, A. A.; and Rasor, R. W. (1953) Psychiatric Aspects Of Drug Addiction AJMed: 14: 566-570.

110. Wieder, H. (1946) Addiction to Meperidine Hydrochloride (Demerol) JAMA: 132: 1066-1068.

111. Wieder, H. (1949) Objective Evaluation of Insulin Therapy of the Morphine Abstinence Syndrome.J. Nerv. and Ment. Dis. Vol: 110: 26-35.

112. Wieder, H. and Kaplan, E. H. (1969) Drug Use in Adolescence: The Psychodynamic Meaning and Pharmacogenic Effect. Psa. Study Child 24: 399-431 IUP.

113. Wieder, H. (1979) Needed: A Theory National Insitute of Drug Abuse(NIDA) Reseach Monograph #12 Psychodynamics of Drug Dependence.

114. Wieder, H. (1978) Pre-adolescence and adolescence in Glenn (22)

115. Wieder, H {1966) Intellectuality PsaStCh XX1:294-323

116. World Book Encyclopedia Hercules

117. Wilkins, L. (1965) The diagnosis and Treatment of Endocrine Disorders of Childhood and Adolescence Springfield: Charles C. Thomas.

118. Wittels, F. (1949) The ego of the adolescent (in) Searchlights on delinquency Iup NY

119. Wurmser, L. (1979) Mr. Pecksniff's Horse Psycho-Dynamics of Drug Use. NIDA Research Monongraph #12 pp. 37-72 May.

120. Wurmser, L. (1970) Why People Take Drugs: escape and search Maryland State Med. J. Nov.